Algebra 2

COMMON CORE State Standards Curriculum Companion

Student Edition

Edward B. Burger
David J. Chard
Paul A. Kennedy
Steven J. Leinwand
Freddie L. Renfro
Tom W. Roby
Bert K. Waits

HOLT McDOUGAL

 HOUGHTON MIFFLIN HARCOURT

Printed in the U.S.A.

ISBN 978-0-547-61816-6

3 4 5 6 7 8 9 10   0877   20 19 18 17 16 15 14 13 12 11

4500305196   B C D E F G

Cover photo: © Art by Vladimir Bulatov/Bulatov Abstract Creations/Photo by Victoria Smith/HMH

COMMON CORE

ALGEBRA 2 COMMON CORE STATE STANDARDS CURRICULUM COMPANION

Student Edition

Contents

Mastering the Standards

for Mathematical Practice

The topics described in the Standards for Mathematical Content will vary from year to year. However, the *way* in which you learn, study, and think about mathematics will not. The Standards for Mathematical Practice describe skills that you will use in all of your math courses.

Mathematical Practices

1. *Make sense of problems and persevere in solving them.*
2. *Reason abstractly and quantitatively.*
3. *Construct viable arguments and critique the reasoning of others.*
4. *Model with mathematics.*
5. *Use appropriate tools strategically.*
6. *Attend to precision.*
7. *Look for and make use of structure.*
8. *Look for and express regularity in repeated reasoning.*

1 Make sense of problems and persevere in solving them.

Mathematically proficient students start by explaining to themselves the meaning of a problem... They analyze givens, constraints, relationships, and goals. They make conjectures about the form... of the solution and plan a solution pathway...

In your book

Focus on Problem Solving describes a four-step plan for problem solving. The plan is introduced at the beginning of your book, and practice with the plan appears throughout the book.

Focus on Problem Solving

The Problem-Solving Plan

To be a good problem solver you need a good problem-solving plan. Using a problem-solving plan along with a problem-solving strategy helps you organize your work and correctly solve the problem. The plan used in this book is outlined below.

UNDERSTAND the Problem

- **What are you asked to find?** Make sure you understand exactly what the problem is asking. Restate the problem in your own words.
- **What information is given in the problem?** List every piece of information the problem gives you.
- **Is all the information relevant?** Sometimes problems have extra information that is not needed to solve the problem. Try to determine what is and is not needed. This helps you stay organized when you are making a plan.
- **Were you given enough information to solve the problem?** Sometimes there simply is not enough information to solve the problem. List what else you need to know to solve the problem.

Make a PLAN

- **What problem-solving strategy or strategies can you use to help you solve the problem?** Think about strategies you have used in the past to solve problems. Would any of them be helpful in solving this problem?
- **Create a step-by-step plan of how you will solve the problem.** Write out your plan in words to help you get a clearer idea of how to solve the problem mathematically.

SOLVE

- **Use your plan to solve the problem.** Translate your plan from words to math. Show each step in your solution and write your answer in a complete sentence.

LOOK BACK

- **Did you completely answer the question that was asked?** Be sure you answered the question that was asked and that your answer is complete.
- **Is your answer reasonable?** Your answer should make sense.
- **Could you have used a different strategy to solve the problem?** Solving the problem again with a different strategy is a good way to check your answer.
- **Did you learn anything that could help you solve similar problems in the future?** You may want to take notes about this kind of problem and the strategy you used to solve it.

xx *Focus On Problem Solving*

PROBLEM SOLVING

Problem-Solving Application

The cost to place an ad in a newspaper for one week is a linear function of the number of lines in the ad. The costs for 3, 5, and 10 lines are shown. Write an equation in slope-intercept form that represents the function. Then find the cost of an ad that is 18 lines long.

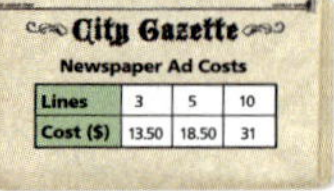

Newspaper Ad Costs

Lines	3	5	10
Cost ($)	13.50	18.50	31

1 Understand the Problem

- The **answer** will have two parts—an equation in slope-intercept form and the cost of an ad that is 18 lines long.
- The ordered pairs given in the table satisfy the equation.

2 Make a Plan

First, find the slope. Then use point-slope form to write the equation. Finally, write the equation in slope-intercept form.

3 Solve

Step 1 Choose any two ordered pairs from the table to find the slope.

$$m = \frac{y_2 - y_1}{x_2 - x_1} = \frac{18.50 - 13.50}{5 - 3} = \frac{5}{2} = 2.5 \quad \textit{Use (3, 13.50) and (5, 18.50).}$$

Step 2 Substitute the slope and any ordered pair from the table into the point-slope form.

$$y - y_1 = m(x - x_1)$$
$$y - 31 = 2.5(x - 10) \quad \textit{Use (10, 31).}$$

Step 3 Write the equation in slope-intercept form by solving for y.

$$y - 31 = 2.5(x - 10)$$
$$y - 31 = 2.5x - 25 \quad \textit{Distribute 2.5.}$$
$$y = 2.5x + 6 \quad \textit{Add 31 to both sides.}$$

Step 4 Find the cost of an ad containing 18 lines by substituting 18 for x.

$$y = 2.5x + 6$$
$$y = 2.5(18) + 6 = 51$$

The cost of an ad containing 18 lines is $51.

4 Look Back

Check the equation by substituting the ordered pairs (3, 13.50) and (5, 18.50).

y	$= 2.5x + 6$
13.50	2.5(3) + 6
13.5	7.5 + 6
13.5	13.5 ✓

y	$= 2.5x + 6$
18.50	2.5(5) + 6
18.5	12.5 + 6
18.5	18.5 ✓

8-3A EXTENSION

Polynomials, Rational Expressions, and Closure

Objective
Understand under which operations rational expressions are closed.

A set of numbers is *closed*, or has closure, under a given operation if the result of the operation on any two numbers in the set is also in the set.

For example, the set of real numbers is closed under addition, because adding any two real numbers results in another real number. Likewise, the real numbers are closed under subtraction, multiplication and division (by a nonzero real number), because performing these operations on two real numbers always yields another real number.

Polynomials are closed under the same operations as integers. Rational expressions are closed under addition, subtraction, multiplication, and division by a nonzero rational expression.

EXAMPLE 1 Determining Closure of the Set of Integers Under Operations

Explain why the integers are closed under the stated operation or give a counterexample to explain why they are not closed under the stated operation.

Addition

For any two integers a and b, the sum of the integers would result in an integer. Looking at a number line and starting at any integer point a, the sum would indicate a move to point b to the left or right using b units, which are integers. The set of integers is closed under addition.

Subtraction

Subtraction can be rewritten as an addition, that is, $a - b = a + (-b)$. Because b is an integer, $-b$ is one too, so integer subtraction is also closed.

Multiplication

The product of a and b, where a and b are integers, will always result in an integer, since multiplication is repeated addition. For example, $2 \cdot 3$ can be written as $2 + 2 + 2$. Since integers are closed under addition, they are also closed under multiplication.

Division

Integers are not closed under division. A counterexample to demonstrate this is $a = 5$ and $b = -4$. The division $a \div b$ would result in the fraction, $-\frac{5}{4}$, which is not an integer.

1. Determine if the set of positive integers is closed under addition, subtraction, multiplication, and division. Explain.

A rational number is any number that can be written as a ratio of two integers. All rational numbers can be written in the form $\frac{a}{b}$, where a and b are integers.

EXAMPLE 2 Determining Closure of the Set of Rational Numbers Under Operations

Explain why the rational numbers are closed under the stated operation or give a counterexample to explain why they are not closed under the stated operation.

Addition

If $\frac{a}{b}$ and $\frac{c}{d}$ are nonzero and a, b, c, and d are integers, then $\frac{a}{b} + \frac{c}{d} = \frac{(ad + bc)}{bd}$. Since integers are closed under addition and the products ad, bc, bd, and $(ad + bc)$ are integers, then the sum of two nonzero rational numbers is a rational number. Therefore the rational numbers are closed under addition.

Subtraction

Since subtraction can be rewritten as an addition, that is, $\frac{a}{b} - \frac{c}{d} = \frac{a}{b} + \left(-\frac{c}{d}\right)$, then rational numbers are also closed under subtraction.

Multiplication

If $\frac{a}{b}$ and $\frac{c}{d}$ are nonzero and a, b, c, and d are integers, then $\frac{a}{b} \cdot \frac{c}{d} = \frac{ac}{bd}$. Since integers are closed under multiplication, then ac and bd are also integers and the fraction is a rational number. Therefore the rational numbers are closed under multiplication.

Division (nonzero)

Since division of two fractions can be rewritten as a multiplication, rational numbers are closed under division. Let $\frac{a}{b}$ and $\frac{c}{d}$ be nonzero and a, b, c, and d be integers, then $\frac{a}{b} \div \frac{c}{d} = \frac{a}{b} \cdot \frac{d}{c} = \frac{ad}{bc}$. Since integers are closed under multiplication, then ad and bc are also integers and the fraction is a rational number. Therefore the rational numbers are closed under (nonzero) division.

2. Determine if the set of negative rational numbers is closed under addition, subtraction, multiplication, and division. Explain.

The operations of polynomials are similar to operations with real numbers. Examples of operations with polynomials are shown below.

Addition

$4t + 6r$
$+[2t - 4r]$
$(4 + 2)t + [6 + (-4)]r$
$6t + 2r$

Combine like terms.

Subtraction

$-4t + 2r$
$-[2t - 4r]$
$(-4 - 2)t + [2 - (-4)]r$
$-6t + 6r$

Combine like terms.

Multiplication

$(x^3 + 3)(-x^2 + x)$
$x^3(-x^2 + x) + 3(-x^2 + x)$
$-x^5 + x^4 - 4x^2 + 3x$

Use the distributive property or FOIL.

Division

$$\begin{array}{r} x + 2 \\ x + 1\overline{)x^2 + 3x + 2} \\ -(x^2 + x) \\ \hline 2x + 2 \\ -(2x + 2) \\ \hline 0 \end{array}$$

EXAMPLE 3 Determining Closure of Polynomials

Explain why polynomials are closed under the stated operation or give a counterexample to explain why they are not closed under the stated operation.

Addition

When combining like terms, real numbers are added. The coefficients are sums of real numbers and the result is therefore real. The powers of variables do not change in addition of polynomials, so the exponents remain whole numbers. Therefore, the set of polynomials is closed under addition with real-number coefficients.

Multiplication

The distributive property is used to multiply each of the terms in each polynomial multiplied. Since the coefficients are multiplied and they are real numbers, their products will also be real numbers. The product of variables with real number exponents m and n results in the same variable with a real exponent $m + n$: $x^m \cdot x^n = x^{m+n}$. The exponents are whole numbers, so the multiplication of polynomials is closed with real-number coefficients and whole-number exponents.

3. Determine if the set of polynomials is closed under subtraction with real-number coefficients.

A rational expression is the ratio of two polynomial expressions. The denominator of a rational expression cannot equal 0, as division by 0 is undefined.

Closure properties for rational expressions can be derived using the closure properties of polynomial expressions, as rational expressions are composed of polynomial expressions.

EXAMPLE 4 Determining Closure of Rational Expressions

Show that rational expressions are closed under addition.

We can consider generic rational expressions $\frac{f(x)}{g(x)}$ and $\frac{p(x)}{q(x)}$, where $f(x)$, $g(x)$, $p(x)$, and $q(x)$ represent polynomials, and $g(x)$ and $q(x)$ are not equal to 0. To add the functions, use a common denominator.

$$\frac{f(x)}{g(x)} + \frac{p(x)}{q(x)} = \left(\frac{f(x)}{g(x)} \cdot \frac{q(x)}{q(x)}\right) + \left(\frac{p(x)}{q(x)} \cdot \frac{g(x)}{g(x)}\right)$$

$$= \left(\frac{f(x) \cdot q(x)}{g(x) \cdot q(x)}\right) + \left(\frac{p(x) \cdot g(x)}{g(x) \cdot q(x)}\right)$$

$$= \frac{\left(f(x) \cdot q(x)\right) + \left(p(x) \cdot g(x)\right)}{\left(g(x) \cdot q(x)\right)}$$

Since the product of two polynomials is a polynomial and the sum of two polynomials is a polynomial, then the sum of two rational expressions is a rational expression.

4. Determine if the set of rational numbers is closed under multiplication.

EXTENSION

Exercises

Determine if each set is closed under the given operation. Explain why the set is closed or provide a counterexample to show the set is not closed.

1. The set of whole numbers; division

2. The set of odd numbers; addition

3. The set of positive even numbers; subtraction

4. The set of multiples of 5; multiplication

5. The set of even integers; addition

6. The set of multiples of 2; division

7. **Challenge** Show that polynomials are closed under subtraction. Explain all steps in your response.

8. **Challenge** Show that rational expressions are closed under division. Explain all steps in your response.

9. ///ERROR ANALYSIS/// David used the following logic to show that the set of integers is closed under division. What is wrong with his logic?

1, 3, and 9 integers.

$\frac{9}{1} = 9$, *which is an integer.*

$\frac{9}{3} = 3$, *which is an integer.*

$\frac{9}{9} = 1$, *which is an integer.*

Since each division results in an integer, the set of integers is closed under division.

10. Show that the set {–1, 1} is closed under division.

11. Show that the set {–1, 1} is closed under multiplication.

12. Is the set {–1, 1} closed under addition and/or subtraction? If yes, show it. If no, provide a counterexample.

13. What is the smallest subset of the integers that is closed under addition?

14. Under how many and which of the four operations discussed in this extension (addition, subtraction, multiplication, and nonzero division) is the set of natural numbers closed?

15. **Challenge** Modular arithmetic is a system of arithmetic where the numbers 'wrap around' after a certain value, called the *modulus*. As an example, think of the 'hour' numbers on a clock: – 12 is considered the same as 0, and after 12, the time wraps back around to 1. Twenty hours after 10:00 is 6:00, not 30:00.

a. What is the modulus on a clock?

b. Is the set of 'clock numbers' closed under addition? Explain.

Mastering the Standards

for Mathematical Practice

The topics described in the Standards for Mathematical Content will vary from year to year. However, the *way* in which you learn, study, and think about mathematics will not. The Standards for Mathematical Practice describe skills that you will use in all of your math courses.

Mathematical Practices

1. *Make sense of problems and persevere in solving them.*
2. *Reason abstractly and quantitatively.*
3. *Construct viable arguments and critique the reasoning of others.*
4. *Model with mathematics.*
5. *Use appropriate tools strategically.*
6. *Attend to precision.*
7. *Look for and make use of structure.*
8. *Look for and express regularity in repeated reasoning.*

4 Model with mathematics.

Mathematically proficient students can apply... mathematics... to... problems... in everyday life, society, and the workplace...

In your book

Multi-Step Test Prep and **Real-World Connections** apply mathematics to other disciplines and in real-world scenarios.

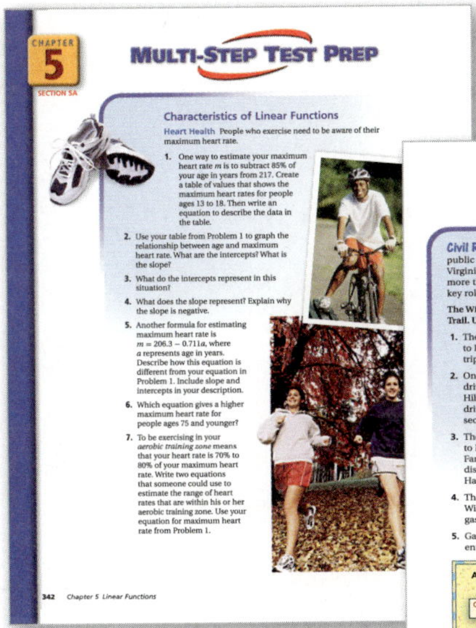

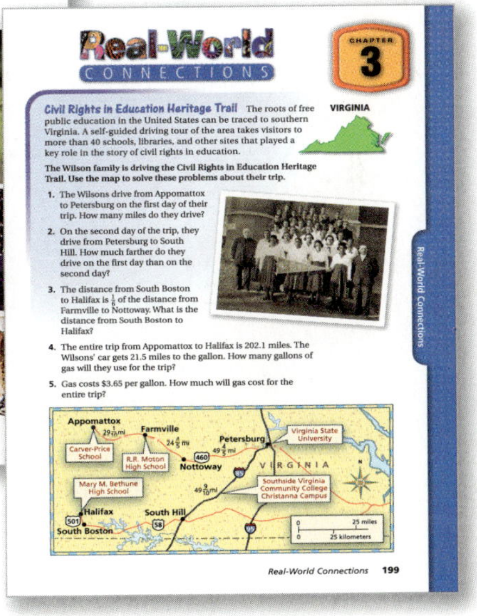

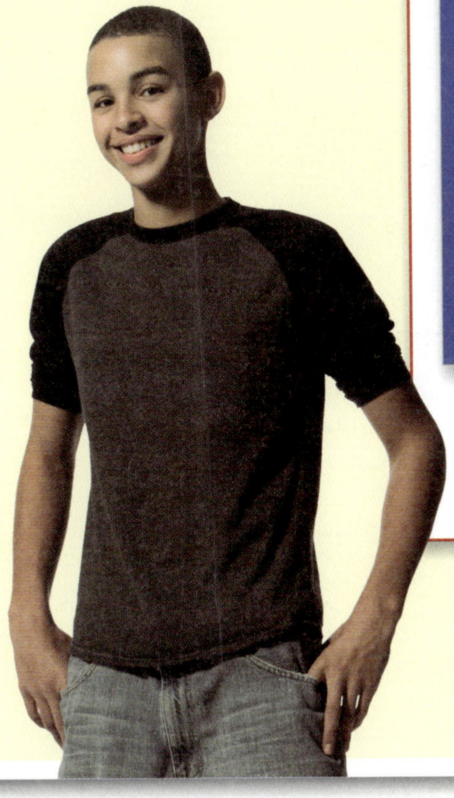

PhotoDisc/Getty Images

8-8A EXTENSION

Solving Equations Graphically

Objective
Solve equations graphically.

Equations can be solved graphically, using the intersection of functions to find the solutions. Each side of the equal sign is graphed as a separate solution, where $f(x) = g(x)$ and the intersection represents the solution.

EXAMPLE 1

Solving Equations Algebraically and Graphically

Solve the equation $5x + 10 = 2x + 31$ algebraically and graphically.

Method 1 Solve the equation algebraically.

$$5x + 10 = 2x + 31$$
$$5x - 2x + 10 = 2x - 2x + 31$$
$$3x + 10 - 10 = 31 - 10$$
$$3x = 21$$
$$x = 7$$

Method 2 Solve the equation graphically. Divide the equation into two equations:

Let $y_1 = 5x + 10$ and $y_2 = 2x + 31$. Graph each equation.

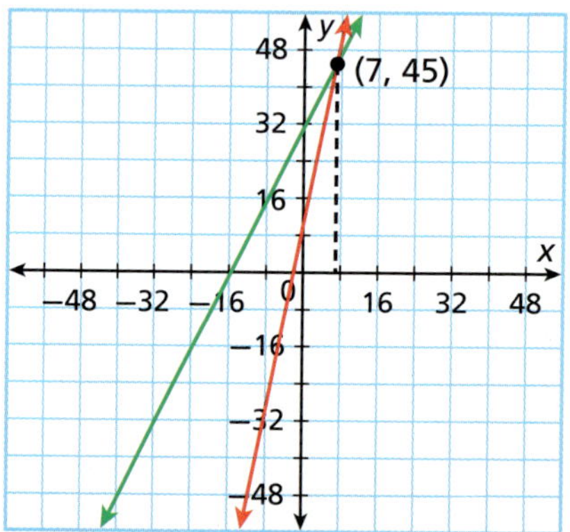

The x-coordinate of the point where the lines intersect is the solution to the equation.

In this case, the solution is $x = 7$. Compare the solution found through graphing to the solution found algebraically. Notice that the solutions are the same, so the solution to the equation $5x + 10 = 2x + 31$.

1. Solve the equation $-3x + 10 = 2x + 5$ algebraically and graphically.

The solutions of the equation $f(x) = g(x)$ are the x-coordinates of the intersections of $y = f(x)$ and $y = g(x)$.

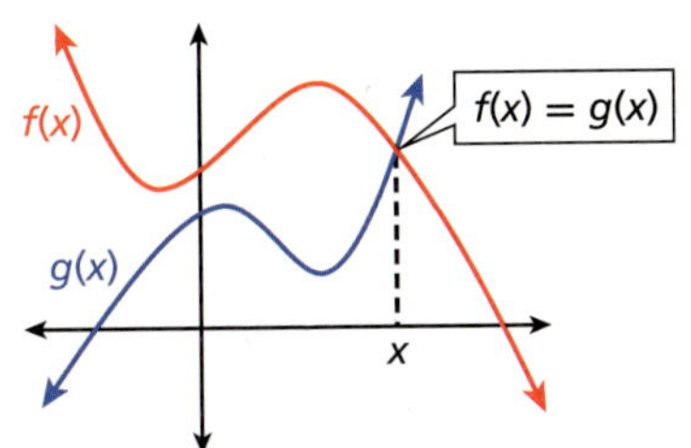

If the graphs do not intersect, there is no solution. If the graphs share every point in common, there are an infinite number of solutions.

EXAMPLE 2 Solving Equations Graphically with the Use of Technology

Solve the equation $x + 2 = -4x + 7$ graphically using technology.

1. Write the equation $x + 2 = -4x + 7$ as two separate equations: $y_1 = x + 2$ and $y_2 = -4x + 7$. Enter each equation into a calculator to graph.
2. Press GRAPH to display the functions.
3. Press TRACE and use the ◀ and ▶ to locate the point of intersection. The X value is the solution to the equation.

Alternatively, you can follow the steps below:

1. Write the equation $x + 2 = -4x + 7$ as two separate equations: $y_1 = x + 2$ and $y_2 = -4x + 7$. Enter each equation into the calculator to graph.
2. Press 2nd TRACE (CALC) and choose Intersect (#5).
3. Select the first line and press ENTER, then select the second line and press ENTER.
4. Arrow to the intersection and press ENTER. The calculator will display the intersection.

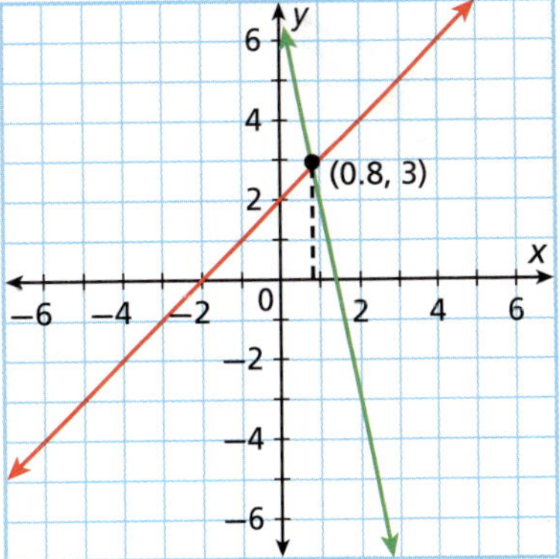

2. Solve the equation $5x + 1 = 2x - 9$ using technology.

EXAMPLE 3 Using a Graphing Calculator Table to Solve

Solve the equation $x^4 + 4 = 5x^2$ graphically using tables.

1. Write the equation $x^4 + 4 = 5x^2$ as two separate equations: $y = x^4 + 4$ and $y = 5x^2$.

2. Press Y=. Enter the first equation, $y = x^4 + 4$, in $\mathbf{Y_1}$ and the second equation, $y = 5x^2$ in $\mathbf{Y_2}$.

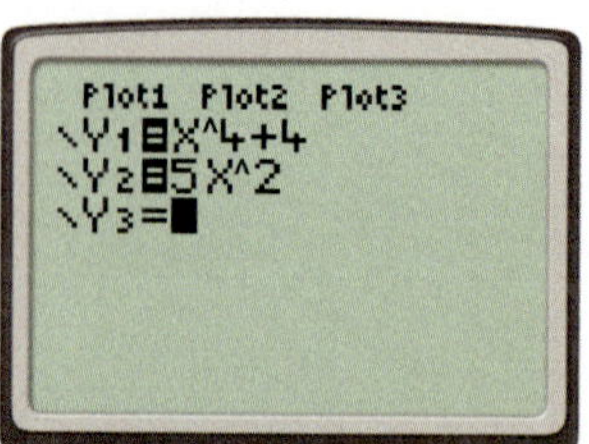

3. Press 2nd GRAPH (TABLE) to use the **TABLE** function.

4. Scroll through the values using ▲ and ▼. Look for values where Y_1 and Y_2 are equal, then find the corresponding X value. The X value is the solution to the equation. Make sure you continue to verify all values to find all possible solutions to the equation.

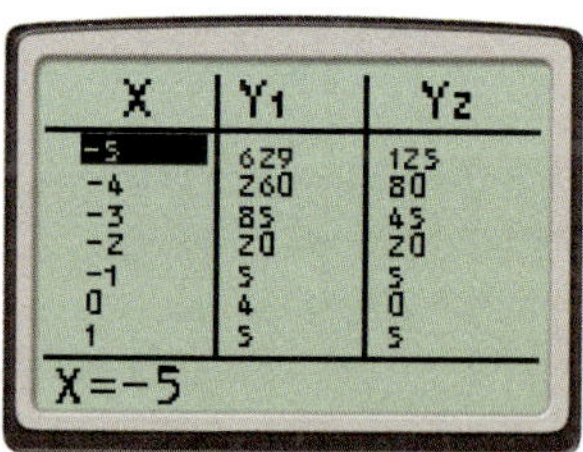

5. Press GRAPH and verify where your lines intersect. The solutions are $x = -2, -1, 1,$ and 2.

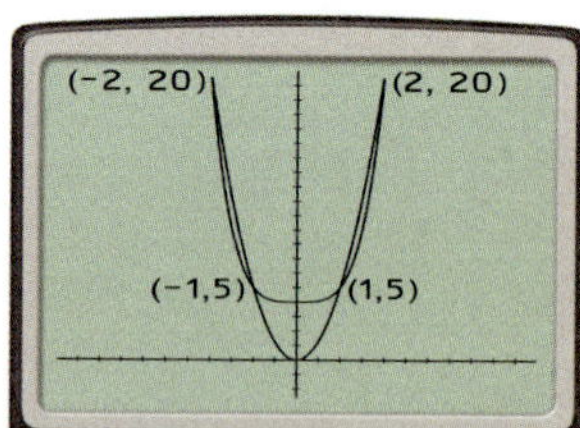

Check

$$x^4 + 4 = 5x^2$$

$$x^4 - 5x^2 + 4 = 0$$

$$(x^2 - 4)(x^2 - 1) = 0$$

$$(x + 2)(x - 2)(x + 1)(x - 1) = 0$$

Helpful Hint

Press 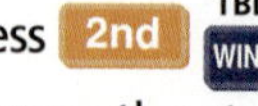 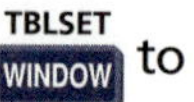 (TBLSET) to change the starting value of the table and the difference between *x*-values. If the graphs intersect between *x*-values in the table, you may not find every solution.

3. Solve the equation $x^2 + 8 = 3x + 6$ graphically using technology.

EXAMPLE 4 Verifying Special Cases Graphically

Use technology to verify graphically that the equation $x^2 - 2x + 3 = -x^2 + 1$ has no solution.

Write the equation as two separate equations: $y_1 = x^2 - 2x + 3$ and $y_2 = -x^2 + 1$. Graph using technology.

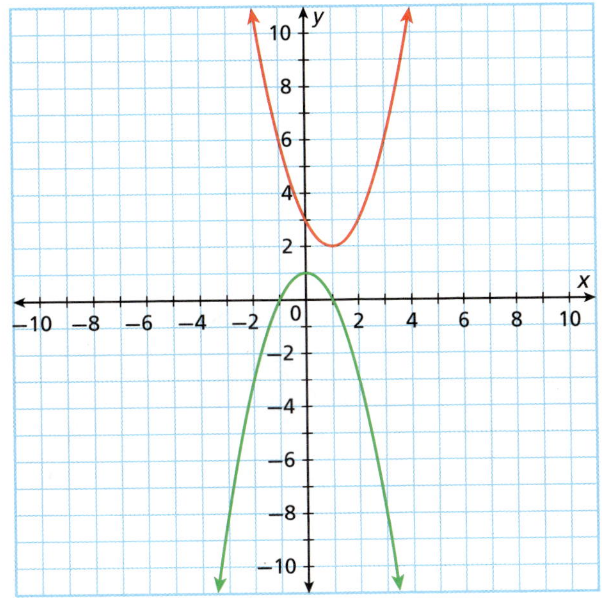

Notice that the graphs don't intersect. Since the graphs will never intersect, regardless of the window chosen to display the graphs, the equation has no solution.

4. Use technology to verify graphically that the equation $4(x^3 - 3) = 4x^3 - 12$ has infinitely many solutions.

EXTENSION Exercises

Solve each equation graphically.

1. $-\frac{1}{2}x + 5 = 3x + 9$

2. $x^5 + 1 = 2x^2 + x - 10$

3. $|x + 2| = x^2$

4. $\frac{1}{x - 8} = x$

5. $\log(x + 1) = -4\log(x)$

6. $e^x = 2e^{3x}$

7. $x^2 = -x^4 - 2$

8. $|x^2 + 1| = |x - 2|$

9. $3x^2 + 6 = 3(x^2 + 2)$

10. $-x^4 - 5x + 2 = x^2 + 7$

11. **Write About It** How do you determine if an equation has undefined values? What should be done if a calculator shows an intersection in a value that should be undefined?

9-1A Comparing Functions

Objective
Compare properties of two functions. Estimate and compare rates of change.

Who uses this?
A real estate developer may use graphs of exponential population growth to decide when and where to invest.

The graph of the exponential function $y = 0.2491e^{0.0081x}$ shows the population growth in Baltimore, Maryland.

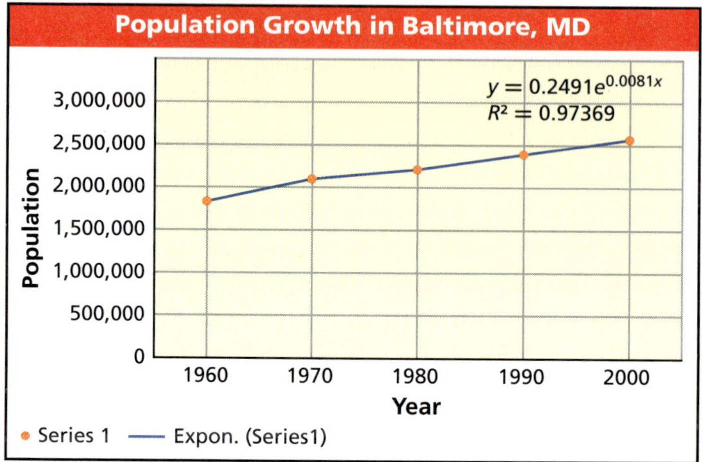

The graph of the exponential function $y = 0.0023e^{0.0089x}$ shows the population growth in Hagerstown, Maryland. The trends can be used to predict what the population will be in the future in each city.

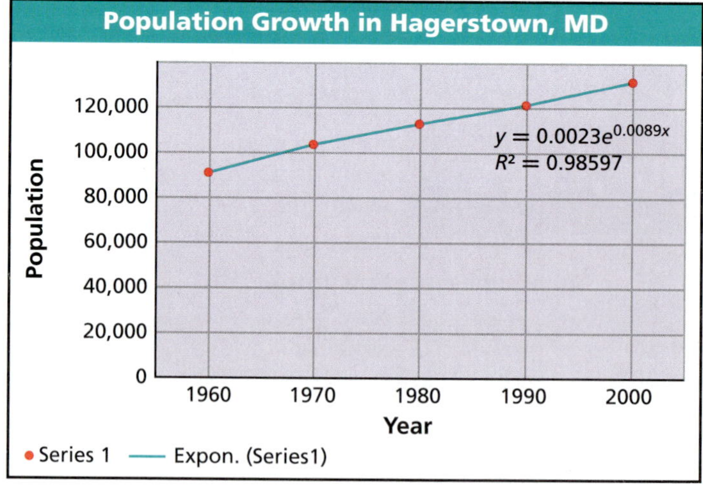

In this lesson, you will compare the graphs of linear, quadratic, and exponential functions.

Minimum and Maximum

A **linear function** will not have a minimum or maximum. A **quadratic function** will have either an absolute minimum or an absolute maximum. Polynomials of degree 3 or higher will have both local and absolute minimum or maximum values.

EXAMPLE 1 Comparing the Average Rate of Change of Two Functions

Katie and Jackie swim laps every day. They each keep track of the time it takes to complete one full lap. The table shows the times it takes Katie to complete 20 laps and the graph shows the time it takes Jackie to complete 20 laps. Find the average rate of change for each set of data. Compare the average rates and explain what the difference in rate of change represents.

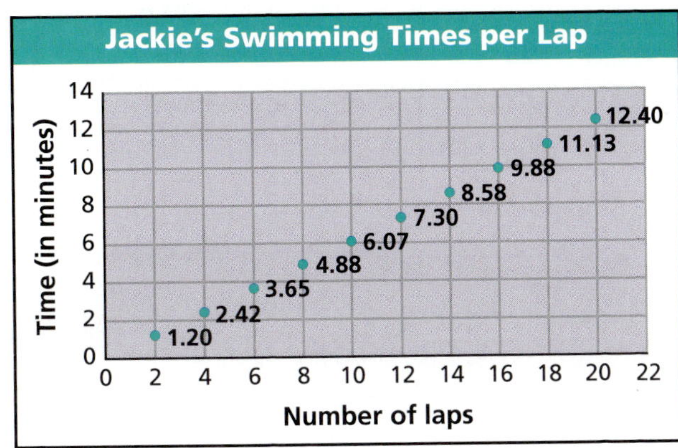

Katie's Swimming Times per Lap	
# of Laps	Time Elapsed (in minutes)
2	1.08
4	2.22
6	3.43
8	4.70
10	5.98
12	7.13
14	8.23
16	9.40
18	10.60
20	11.77

Step 1 Find the average rate of change for each of the data sets.

Rate of change for Jackie's data: $m = \frac{y_2 - y_1}{x_2 - x_1} = \frac{12.40 - 1.2}{20 - 2} \approx 0.62$

Rate of change for Katie's data: $m = \frac{y_2 - y_1}{x_2 - x_1} = \frac{11.77 - 1.08}{20 - 2} \approx 0.59$

Step 2 Compare the rates and interpret the data.

Katie's rate of change is less than Jackie's rate of change. In this case, the rate of change represents the average speed per lap, so Katie has a faster average speed per lap than Jackie.

Helpful Hint

Remember, to find the average rate of change over a data set, find the slope between the first and last data point. To review how to find slope, see page 116.

1. John and Mike opened savings accounts on the same day. They did not deposit any money initially, but deposited each week as shown by the graph and the table. Compare the average rates of change and explain what the rates represent in this situation.

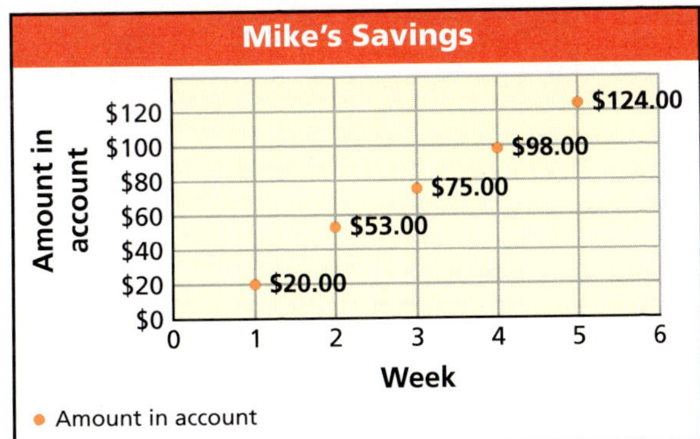

John's Savings	
Week	Amount in Account
1	$25.00
3	$86.00
4	$106.00
5	$130.00
8	$204.00

EXAMPLE 2 Sketching Graphs of Functions Given Key Features

Saul launched an object from the ground. The graph for the height of the object, $h(t)$, in feet after t seconds passes through the points (0, 0), (2, 3.2), and (−4, −124). Sketch a graph of the quadratic equation that models the situation. Find the point that represents the maximum height of the object.

Step 1 Use the points to find the values of a, b, and c in the function $h(t) = at^2 + bt + c$.

$(t, h(t))$	$h(t) = at^2 + bt + c$	System in a, b, c
(0, 0)	$0 = a(0)^2 + b(0) + c$	$0 = c$
(2, 3.2)	$3.2 = a(2)^2 + b(2) + c$	$3.2 = 4a + 2b + c$
(−4, −124)	$-124 = a(-4)^2 + b(-4) + c$	$-124 = 16a - 4b + c$

Step 2 Solve the system found in Step 1 and write the equation.

$$\begin{cases} 0 = c \\ 3.2 = 4a + 2b + c \\ -124 = 16a - 4b + c \end{cases}$$

$$\begin{cases} 3.2 = 4a + 2b + 0 \\ -124 = 16a - 4b + 0 \end{cases}$$

Substitute $c = 0$ in 2nd and 3rd equation.

$$\begin{cases} 6.4 = 8a + 4b \\ -124 = 16a - 4b \end{cases}$$

Multiply the first equation by 2 in order to use elimination.

$$-117.6 = 24a$$

Add equations and solve.

$$-4.9 = a$$

$$3.2 = 4(-4.9) + 2b + 0$$

$$3.2 = -19.6 + 2b$$

$$11.4 = b$$

$$h(t) = -4.9t^2 + 11.4t$$

Helpful Hint

Remember, in the equation $f(x) = a(x - h)^2 + k$, the point (h, k) represents the vertex, see page 116.

Step 3 Find the maximum height of the function by finding the vertex. Graph the function and approximate the vertex.

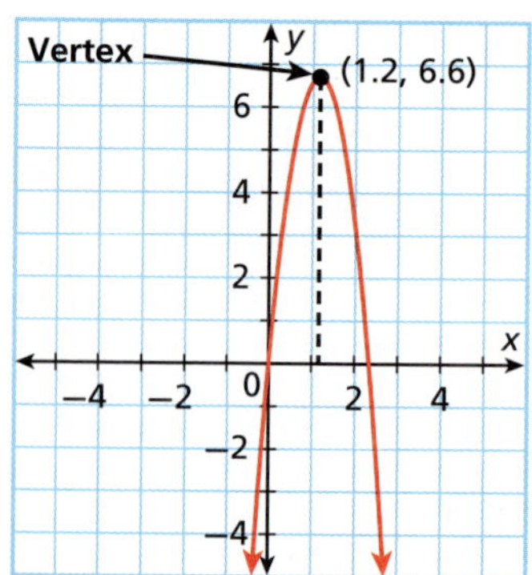

The maximum height of the object is approximately 6.62 feet.

2. The table shows the profit for a company. Find and graph the cubic function that describes the data.

x	2004	2005	2006	2007	2008
y	324,500	382,000	495,500	670,500	912,500

EXAMPLE 3

Comparing Exponential and Polynomial Functions

Compare the end behavior of the functions $f(x) = 3^x$ and $g(x) = x^4$.

Graph each of the functions.

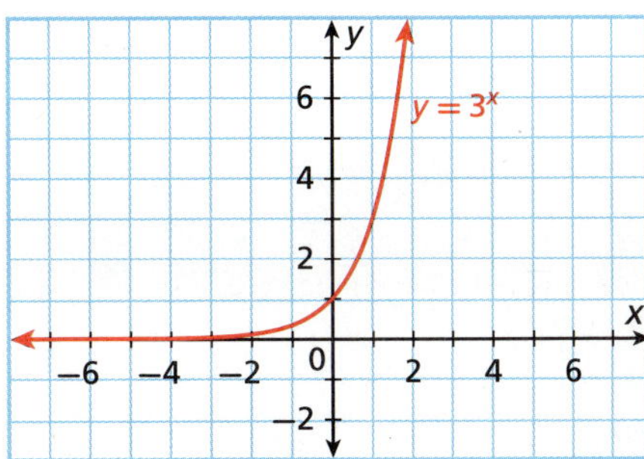

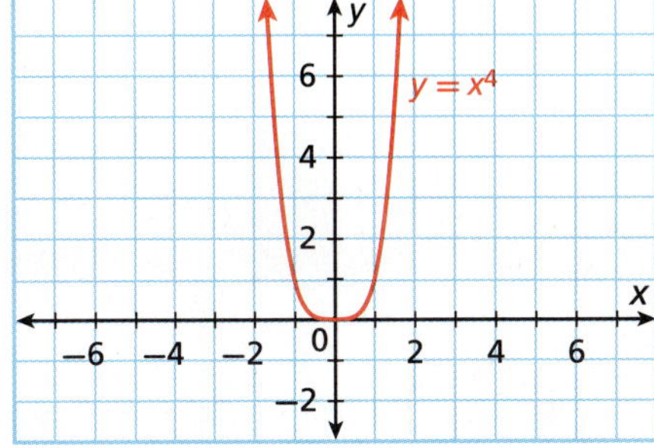

The end behavior for the graph of $f(x) = 3^x$:

As x approaches positive infinity, $f(x)$ approaches positive infinity. As x approaches negative infinity, $f(x)$ approaches 0.

The end behavior for the graph of $g(x) = x^4$:

As x approaches positive infinity, $f(x)$ approaches positive infinity. As x approaches negative infinity, $f(x)$ approaches positive infinity.

3. Compare the end behavior of the functions $f(x) = 4x^2$ and $g(x) = x^3$.

Exponential Function End Behavior

Base $a > 0$

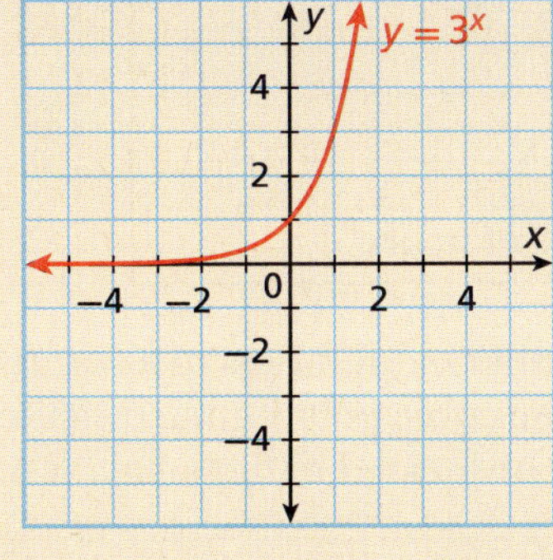

Base $a < 0$

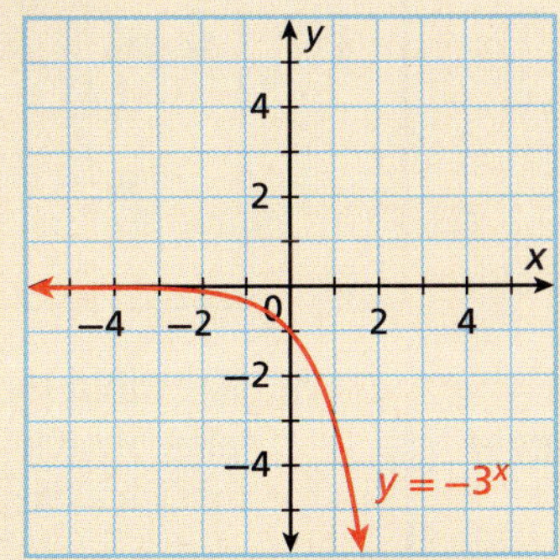

As $x \to +\infty$	As $x \to -\infty$	As $x \to +\infty$	As $x \to -\infty$
$P(x) \to +\infty$	$P(x) \to 0$	$P(x) \to -\infty$	$P(x) \to 0$

THINK AND DISCUSS

1. Explain how to find the average rate of change for a polynomial function.
2. Describe a situation that could be modeled by the function $f(x) = 5x + 25.50$.
3. **GET ORGANIZED** Copy and complete the graphic organizer at right. In each cell, write an example of an equation that satisfies the given end behavior.

		Type of Function
Leading Coefficient $a > 0$	As $x \to +\infty$ $P(x) \to +\infty$ As $x \to -\infty$ $P(x) \to -\infty$	
Leading Coefficient $a < 0$	As $x \to -\infty$ $P(x) \to -\infty$ As $x \to +\infty$ $P(x) \to -\infty$	

9-1A Exercises

GUIDED PRACTICE

1. **Vocabulary** Does the *slope* always represent a rate of change? Explain.

SEE EXAMPLE 1 p. CC11

2. The cost of renting a pedal boat is shown for Company A and Company B below. Compare the y-intercept and hourly rates of each function. Explain what the y-intercept represents in this situation.

Ariel Skelley/Getty Images

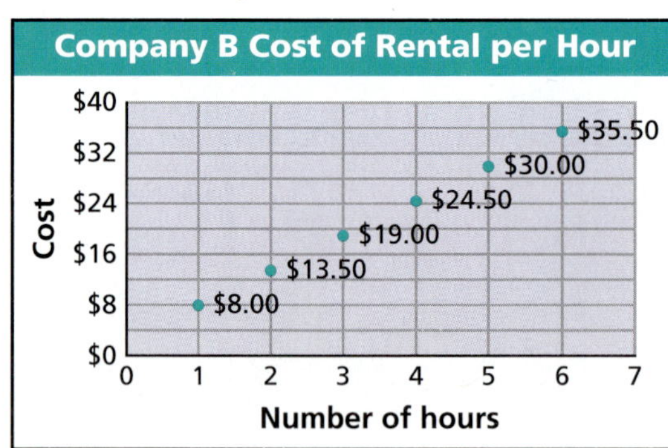

Company A	
Number of Hours	**Cost**
0.5	$7.25
1.0	$8.50
1.5	$9.75
2.0	$11.00
2.5	$12.25
3.0	$13.50

SEE EXAMPLE 2 p. CC12

3. The table shows the number of members of a community volunteer group per year. Sketch a graph of the cubic polynomial function. Find the year where the first local maximum will be located if the behavior of the graph remains the same.

Year	2002	2003	2004	2005	2006	2007
Number of Members	12	45	69	85	94	97

SEE EXAMPLE 3 p. CC13

4. Compare the end behavior of the functions $f(x) = -2^x$ and $f(x) = e^x$.

PRACTICE AND PROBLEM SOLVING

Independent Practice	
For Exercises	See Example
5	1
6	2
7–10	3

5. The monthly rental programs offered by each of two online video rental companies are shown in the graph and table below. What is the least number of rentals for which Company A would offer the best rate?

Company A Rental Program

Cost: $15.00, $12.00, $9.00, $6.00, $3.00, 0

Number of rentals: 0, 1, 2, 3, 4, 5, 6

$10.75, $11.50, $12.25, $13.00, $13.75, $14.50

Company B	
Number of Rentals	Cost
2	$8.00
4	$11.00
6	$14.00
8	$17.00
10	$20.00
12	$23.00

6. Estimation The table shows the height of an object, $h(t)$, in meters after t seconds. Sketch a graph of the quadratic polynomial function. Using the graph, find the approximate time, to the nearest hundredth of a second, after which the object will reach its maximum height.

h(t)	1	2	3	4	5	6
t	138.5	147.2	146.1	135.2	114.5	84

Compare the end behavior for each pair of functions.

7. $f(x) = -3x + 4$ and $g(x) = \log 3^x$

8. $f(x) = \sqrt{x}$ and $g(x) = x^2$

9. $f(x) = -e^{2x}$ and $g(x) = 2\log x$

10. $f(x) = -x^3$ and $g(x) = -x^4$

Find the function which matches the graphical representation shown.

11.

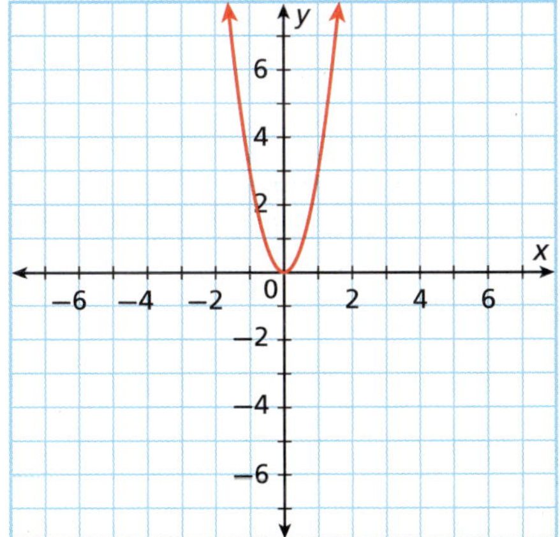

12.

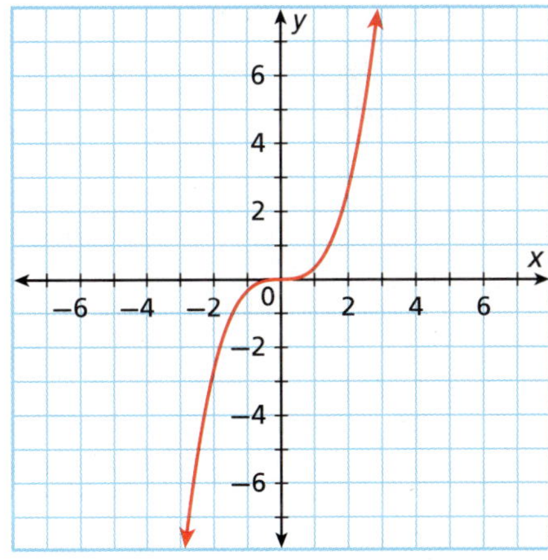

13. Below are two equations. Find the maximum of each, and classify each maximum as absolute maximum or local maximum.

$$f(x) = 3 - (x + 5)^2 \qquad g(x) = x^3 - x^2$$

Find the end behavior of the functions.

14. $f(x) = \frac{1}{2}x^5$

15. $f(x) = -e^x$

16. $f(x) = -6^x$

17. $f(x) = 4x^4 + 3$

18. Write About It Polynomial function graphs have similarities depending on their degree. Explain how you can determine the best regression for using finite differences. Then determine the end behavior of the graph based on the degree of a function and information gathered from a data table.

19. Ann and Jo are taking a road trip. The first day, Ann drives. The second day, Jo drives. Their hourly progress for the two days is shown in the table. Use a graph to compare Ann's and Jo's hourly progress and explain what the slope represents in this situation.

Time (hours)		1	2	3	4	5	6
Distance traveled (miles)	Ann	62	124	186	248	310	372
	Jo	58	116	174	232	290	348

20. Multi-Step An initial population of bacteria contains 500 bacteria. The population growth rate is 3.5%. The function $N(t) = 500e^{0.035t}$ gives the population N at time t.

a. Graph the function for the population growth.

b. What does the y-intercept represent for this function?

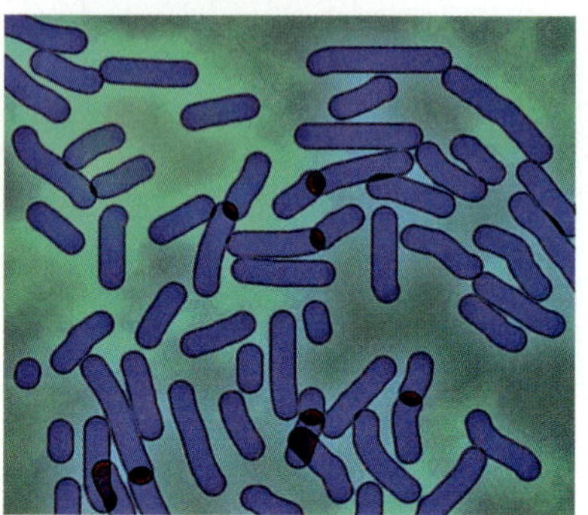
Enigma/Alamy

21. Critical Thinking Compare the end behavior of the logarithmic functions $f(x) = 3\log x$, $g(x) = \log(3x)$, and $h(x) = \log\left(x^3\right)$.

22. ERROR ANALYSIS John determined that the average rate of change for the functions $f(x) = 3(x+5)$ and $h(x) = 3\left(\frac{1}{3}x-5\right)$ are the same. Explain the error.

23. What is the degree of the polynomial best suited for the data below, based on finite differences?

x	4	5	6	7	8
$f(x)$	5	11	18	26	35

Ⓐ linear

Ⓑ quadratic

Ⓒ cubic

Ⓓ quartic

24. Which of the following describes the end behavior of the function $h(x) = 0.2x^5 + 5$?

Ⓐ As $x \to +\infty$, $f(x) \to +\infty$ and as $x \to -\infty$, $f(x) \to -\infty$

Ⓑ As $x \to +\infty$, $f(x) \to -\infty$ and as $x \to -\infty$, $f(x) \to +\infty$

Ⓒ As $x \to +\infty$, $f(x) \to +\infty$ and as $x \to -\infty$, $f(x) \to +\infty$

Ⓓ As $x \to +\infty$, $f(x) \to -\infty$ and as $x \to -\infty$, $f(x) \to -\infty$

25. Which of the following equations has the largest positive rate of change?

Ⓐ $4y + x = 1$

Ⓑ $y + x = -\frac{1}{3}x + 8$

Ⓒ $5y - 10x = 3$

Ⓓ $2y + x = 10$

CHALLENGE AND EXTEND

26. Two car rental companies use different rates per week. The table shows the data for Company A and the graph shows the data for Company B. Compare the y-intercepts and the rates per mile for each of the companies. Which company would you choose if you were renting a car for 1 week? Which would you choose for 4 weeks? Explain your response.

Company A	
Number of Weeks	Cost
1.0	$79.00
2.0	$158.00
3.0	$237.00
4.0	$316.00
5.0	$395.00
6.0	$474.00

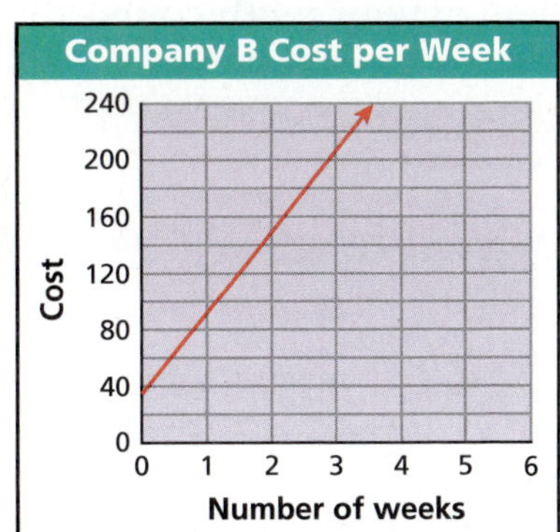

SPIRAL REVIEW

Find the determinant of each matrix. *(Lesson 4-4)*

27. $\begin{bmatrix} -1 & 4 \\ 2 & 3 \end{bmatrix}$

28. $\begin{bmatrix} 2 & -9 \\ 3 & 4 \end{bmatrix}$

29. $\begin{bmatrix} 1 & 2 & 3 \\ 2 & -1 & -2 \\ -1 & 4 & 2 \end{bmatrix}$

30. $\begin{bmatrix} 5 & 6 & 2 \\ 1 & 7 & -3 \\ 1 & 1 & 2 \end{bmatrix}$

Find the zeros of each function by using the quadratic formula. *(Lesson 5-6)*

31. $f(x) = x^2 + 9x + 18$

32. $f(x) = -2x^2 + 16x - 30$

Simplify, if possible. *(Lesson 7-4)*

33. $\log_4 4^2$

34. $\log_3 2187$

Simplify. Identify any x values for which the expression is undefined. *(Lesson 8-2)*

35. $\dfrac{x+2}{4x^2 - 16}$

36. $\dfrac{x+1}{x^2 + 5x + 4}$

37. $\dfrac{11x^2 - 99}{x - 3}$

38. $\dfrac{5x^2 + 25x + 30}{x + 2}$

Mastering the *Standards*

for Mathematical Practice

The topics described in the Standards for Mathematical Content will vary from year to year. However, the *way* in which you learn, study, and think about mathematics will not. The Standards for Mathematical Practice describe skills that you will use in all of your math courses.

Mathematical Practices

1. *Make sense of problems and persevere in solving them.*
2. *Reason abstractly and quantitatively.*
3. *Construct viable arguments and critique the reasoning of others.*
4. *Model with mathematics.*
5. *Use appropriate tools strategically.*
6. *Attend to precision.*
7. *Look for and make use of structure.*
8. *Look for and express regularity in repeated reasoning.*

⑤ Use appropriate tools strategically.

Mathematically proficient students consider the available tools when solving a... problem... [and] are... able to use technological tools to explore and deepen their understanding...

In your book

Algebra Labs and **Technology Labs** use concrete and technological tools to explore mathematical concepts.

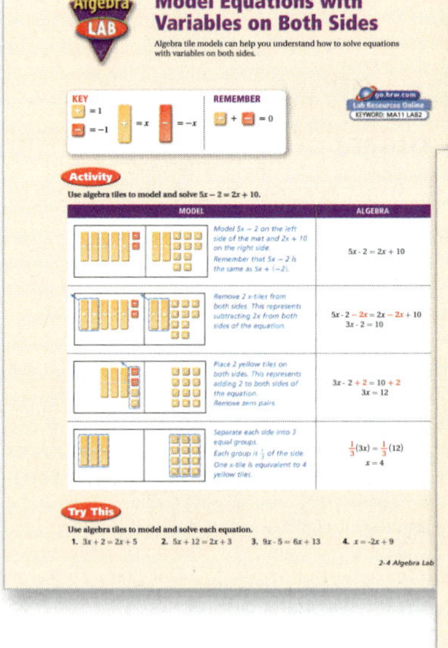

2-4 Algebra LAB

Model Equations with Variables on Both Sides

Algebra tile models can help you understand how to solve equations with variables on both sides.

KEY: = 1; = −1; = x; = $-x$

REMEMBER: + = 0

go.hrw.com Lab Resources Online KEYWORD: MA11 LAB2

Activity

Use algebra tiles to model and solve $5x - 2 = 2x + 10$.

MODEL	ALGEBRA
Model $5x - 2$ on the left side of the mat and $2x + 10$ on the right side. Remember that $5x - 2$ is the same as $5x + (-2)$.	$5x - 2 = 2x + 10$
Remove 2 x-tiles from both sides. This represents subtracting 2x from both sides of the equation.	$5x - 2 - 2x = 2x - 2x + 10$ $3x - 2 = 10$
Place 2 yellow tiles on both sides. This represents adding 2 to both sides of the equation. Remove zero pairs.	$3x - 2 + 2 = 10 + 2$ $3x = 12$
Separate each side into 3 equal groups. Each group is $\frac{1}{3}$ of the side. One x-tile is equivalent to 4 yellow tiles.	$\frac{1}{3}(3x) = \frac{1}{3}(12)$ $x = 4$

Try This

Use algebra tiles to model and solve each equation.

1. $3x + 2 = 2x + 5$ 2. $5x + 12 = 2x + 3$ 3. $9x - 5 = 6x + 13$ 4. $x = -2x + 9$

2-4 Algebra Lab

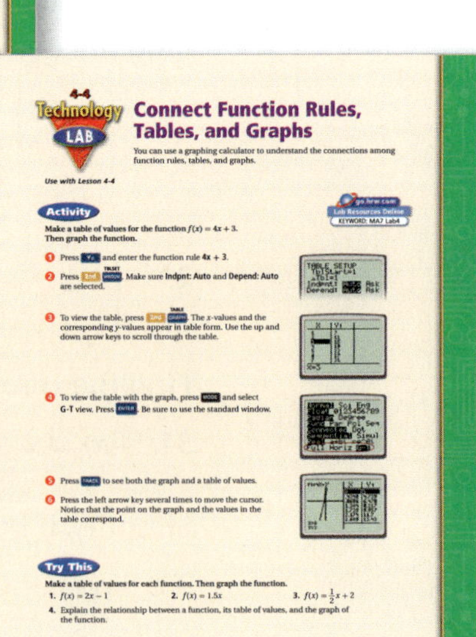

4-4 Technology LAB

Connect Function Rules, Tables, and Graphs

You can use a graphing calculator to understand the connections among function rules, tables, and graphs.

Use with Lesson 4-4

go.hrw.com Lab Resources Online KEYWORD: MA7 Lab4

Activity

Make a table of values for the function $f(x) = 4x + 3$. Then graph the function.

1. Press and enter the function rule **4x + 3**.
2. Press . Make sure **Indpnt: Auto** and **Depend: Auto** are selected.
3. To view the table, press . The x-values and the corresponding y-values appear in table form. Use the up and down arrow keys to scroll through the table.
4. To view the table with the graph, press and select **G-T** view. Press . Be sure to use the standard window.
5. Press to see both the graph and a table of values.
6. Press the left arrow key several times to move the cursor. Notice that the point on the graph and the values in the table correspond.

Try This

Make a table of values for each function. Then graph the function.

1. $f(x) = 2x - 1$ 2. $f(x) = 1.5x$ 3. $f(x) = \frac{1}{2}x + 2$
4. Explain the relationship between a function, its table of values, and the graph of the function.

4-4 Technology Lab 263

11-3A Two-Way Tables

Photodisc/Getty Images

Objectives

Construct and interpret two-way frequency tables of data when two categories are associated with each object being classified.

Vocabulary

joint relative frequency
marginal relative frequency
conditional relative frequency

Who uses this?

Commuters can use two-way tables to determine the best route to work. (See Example 3.)

A *two-way table* is a useful way to organize data that can be categorized by two variables. Suppose you asked 20 children and adults whether they liked broccoli. The table shows one way to arrange the data.

	Yes	No
Children	3	8
Adults	7	2

The **joint relative frequencies** are the values in each category divided by the total number of values, shown by the shaded cells in the table. Each value is divided by 20, the total number of individuals.

The **marginal relative frequencies** are found by adding the joint relative frequencies in each row and column.

	Yes	No	Total
Children	0.15	0.4	0.55
Adults	0.35	0.1	0.45
Total	0.5	0.5	1

EXAMPLE  **1**

Finding Joint and Marginal Relative Frequencies

The table shows the results of a poll of 80 randomly selected high school students who were asked if they prefer math or English. Make a table of the joint and marginal relative frequencies.

	9th grade	10th grade	11th grade	12th grade
Math	10	12	11	8
English	12	11	8	8

Divide each value by the total of 80 to find the joint relative frequencies, and add each row and column to find the marginal relative frequencies.

	9th grade	10th grade	11th grade	12th grade	Total
Math	0.125	0.15	0.1375	0.1	0.5125
English	0.15	0.1375	0.1	0.1	0.4875
Total	0.275	0.2875	0.2375	0.2	1

1. The table shows the number of books sold at a library sale. Make a table of the joint and marginal relative frequencies.

	Fiction	Nonfiction
Hardcover	28	52
Paperback	94	36

To find a **conditional relative frequency**, divide the joint relative frequency by the marginal relative frequency. Conditional relative frequencies can be used to find conditional probabilities.

EXAMPLE 2 Using Conditional Relative Frequency to Find Probability

A sociologist collected data on the types of pets in 100 randomly selected households, and summarized the results in a table.

		Owns a cat	
		Yes	No
Owns a dog	Yes	15	24
	No	18	43

A **Make a table of the joint and marginal relative frequencies.**

		Owns a cat		
		Yes	No	Total
Owns a dog	Yes	0.15	0.24	0.39
	No	0.18	0.43	0.61
	Total	0.33	0.67	1

Idamini/Alamy

B **If you are given that a household has a dog, what is the probability that the household also has a cat?**

Use the conditional relative frequency for the row with the condition "Owns a dog." The total for households with dogs is 0.39, or 39%. Out of these, 0.15, or 15%, also have cats. The conditional relative frequency is $\frac{0.15}{0.39} \approx 0.38$.

Given that a household has a dog, there is a probability of about 0.38 that the household also has a cat.

The classes at a dance academy include ballet and tap dancing. Enrollment in these classes is shown in the table.

		Ballet	
		Yes	No
Tap	Yes	38	52
	No	86	24

2a. Copy and complete the table of the joint relative frequencies and marginal relative frequencies.

		Ballet		
		Yes	No	Total
Tap	Yes			
	No			
	Total			1

2b. If you are given that a student is taking ballet, what is the probability that the student is not taking tap?

Notice that in Example 2, the conditional relative frequency could have been found from the original data:

$$\frac{0.15}{0.39} = \frac{15}{39} \approx 0.38$$

EXAMPLE 3 Comparing Conditional Probabilities

Tomas is trying to decide on the best possible route to drive to work. He has a choice of three possible routes. On each day, he randomly selects a route and keeps track of whether he is late. After a 40-day trial, his notes look like this.

	Late	Not Late
Route A	𝍷𝍷𝍷𝍷	𝍸 𝍸
Route B	𝍷𝍷𝍷	𝍸 𝍷𝍷
Route C	𝍷𝍷𝍷𝍷	𝍸 𝍸 𝍷𝍷

Use conditional probabilities to determine the best route for Tomas to take to work.

Create a table of joint and marginal relative frequencies. There are 40 data values, so divide each frequency by 40.

	Late	Not late	Total
Route A	0.1	0.25	0.35
Route B	0.075	0.175	0.25
Route C	0.1	0.3	0.4
Total	0.275	0.725	1

To find the conditional probabilities, divide the joint relative frequency of being late by the marginal relative frequency in each row.

$P(\text{being late if driving Route A}) = \frac{0.1}{0.35} \approx 0.29$

$P(\text{being late if driving Route B}) = \frac{0.075}{0.25} = 0.3$

$P(\text{being late if driving Route C}) = \frac{0.1}{0.4} = 0.25$

The probability of being late is least for Route C. Based on the sample, Tomas is least likely to be late if he takes Route C.

3. Francine is evaluating three driving schools. She asked 50 people who attended the schools whether they passed their driving tests on the first try.

Use conditional probabilities to determine which is the best school.

	Pass	Fail
Al's Driving	𝍸 𝍸 𝍷𝍷𝍷𝍷	𝍸 𝍷𝍷𝍷
Drive Time	𝍸 𝍸 𝍷	𝍸 𝍷𝍷
Crash Course	𝍸	𝍸

THINK AND DISCUSS

1. Describe the relationship between joint relative frequencies and marginal relative frequencies.

2. Explain how to find the conditional relative frequencies from a two-way table showing joint and marginal relative frequencies.

3. GET ORGANIZED Copy and complete the graphic organizer at right. In each column, explain how to find the relative frequency from a two-way table.

Relative Frequencies		
Joint	Marginal	Conditional

11-3A Exercises

GUIDED PRACTICE

Vocabulary **Apply the vocabulary from this lesson to answer each question.**

1. The ___?___ relative frequencies are the sums of each row and column in a two-way table. (*joint, marginal,* or *conditional*)

2. You can compare ___?___ probabilities to evaluate the best one out of a number of options. (*joint, marginal,* or *conditional*)

SEE EXAMPLE 1
p. CC19

3. The table shows the results of a poll of randomly selected high school students who were asked if they prefer to hear all-school announcements in the morning or afternoon.

	Underclassmen	Upperclassmen
Morning	8	14
Afternoon	18	10

Make a table of the joint and marginal relative frequencies.

4. **Customer Service** The table shows the results of a customer satisfaction survey for a cellular service provider, by location of the customer. In the survey, customers were asked whether they would recommend a plan with the provider to a friend.

	Arlington	Towson	Parkville
Yes	40	35	41
No	18	10	6

Make a table of the joint and marginal relative frequencies. Round to the nearest hundredth where appropriate.

SEE EXAMPLE 2
p. CC20

5. **School** Pamela has collected data on the number of students in the sophomore class who play a sport or play a musical instrument.

Plays an instrument	Plays a sport: Yes	Plays a sport: No
Yes	47	38
No	51	67

Artville/Getty Images

a. Copy and complete the table of the joint and marginal relative frequencies. Round to the nearest hundredth where appropriate.

Play instrument	Play Sport: Yes	Play Sport: No	Total
Yes			
No			
Total			

b. If you are given that a student plays an instrument, what is the probability that the student also plays a sport? Round your answer to the nearest hundredth.

c. If you are given that a student plays a sport, what is the probability that the student also plays an instrument? Round your answer to the nearest hundredth.

SEE EXAMPLE 3
p. CC21

6. **Business** Roberto is the owner of a car dealership. He is assessing the success rates of his top three salespeople in order to offer one of them a promotion. Over two months, for each attempted sale, he records whether the salesperson made a successful sale or not. The results are shown in the chart below.

	Successful	Unsuccessful
Becky	6	6
Raul	4	5
Darrell	6	9

 a. Make a table of the joint relative frequencies and marginal relative frequencies. Round to the nearest hundredth where appropriate.
 b. Find the probability that each salesperson will make a successful sale. Round to the nearest hundredth where appropriate.
 c. Determine which salesperson has the highest success rate.

PRACTICE AND PROBLEM SOLVING

Independent Practice	
For Exercises	See Example
7–8	1
9–12	2
13	3

7. **Fundraising** The table shows the number of T-shirts and sweatshirts sold at a fundraiser during parent visitation night at Preston High School.

	Students	Adults
T-Shirts	16	23
Sweatshirts	7	14

Make a table of the joint relative frequencies and marginal relative frequencies.

8. **Write About It** Describe in your own words the process you use to write marginal relative frequencies for data given in a two-way table.

9. **Customer Service** The claims handlers at a car insurance company help customers with insurance issues when there has been an accident, so their customer service skills are very important.

The claims handlers at the Trust Auto Insurance Company are divided into three teams. For one month, a customer satisfaction survey was given for each team. The results of the surveys are shown below.

	Satisfied	Dissatisfied
Team 1	20	8
Team 2	34	12
Team 3	34	10

 a. Make a table of the joint relative frequencies and marginal relative frequencies. Round to the nearest hundredth where appropriate.
 b. Find the probability that a customer will be satisfied after working with each team. Round to the nearest hundredth where appropriate.
 c. Determine which team has the highest rate of customer satisfaction.

10. **Critical Thinking** What do you notice about the value that always falls in the cell to the lower right of a two-way table when marginal relative frequencies have been written in? What does this value represent?

11. **ERROR ANALYSIS** One hundred adults and children were randomly selected and asked whether they spoke more than one language fluently. The data were recorded in a two-way table. Maria and Brennan each used the data to make the tables of joint relative frequencies shown below, but their results are slightly different. The difference is shaded. Can you tell by looking at the tables which of them made an error? Explain.

Maria's table

	Yes	No
Children	0.15	0.25
Adults	0.1	0.6

Brennan's table

	Yes	No
Children	0.15	0.25
Adults	0.1	0.5

12. **Estimation** A total of 107 brownies and muffins was sold at a school bake sale. The joint relative frequency representing muffins sold to seniors was 0.48. Use mental math to find approximately how many muffins were sold to seniors.

13. **Public Transit** A town planning committee is considering a new system for public transit. Residents of the town were randomly selected to answer two questions: "Do you work within 5 miles of your home?" and "Would you use the new system to get to work, if it were available?"
The results are shown below.

		Work less than 5 miles from home?	
		Yes	No
Use new system?	Yes	24	32
	No	44	20

UpperCut Images/Getty Images

a. Make a table of the joint relative frequencies and marginal relative frequencies. Round to the nearest hundredth where appropriate.

b. If residents work less than 5 miles from home, what is the probability that they would use the new system? Round to the nearest hundredth.

c. If residents are willing to use the new system, what is the probability that they don't work less than 5 miles from home? Round to the nearest hundredth.

14. Students and teachers at a school were polled to see if they were in favor of extending the parking lot into part of the athletic fields. The results of the poll are shown in the two-way table.

	In Favor	Not in Favor
Students	16	23
Teachers	9	14

Which of the following statements is false?

(A) Thirty-nine students were polled in all.

(B) Fourteen teachers were polled in all.

(C) Twenty-three students are not in favor of extending the parking lot.

(D) Nine teachers are in favor of extending the parking lot.

15. A group of students were polled to find out how many were planning to major in a scientific field of study in college. The results of the poll are shown in the two-way table.

		Majoring in a science field	
		Yes	No
Class	Junior	150	210
	Senior	112	200

Which of the following statements is true?

(A) Three hundred sixty students were polled in all.

(B) A student in the senior class is more likely to be planning on a scientific major than a nonscientific major.

(C) A student planning on a scientific major is more likely to be a junior than a senior.

(D) More seniors than juniors plan to enter a scientific field of study.

16. **Gridded Response** A group of children and adults were polled about whether they watch a particular TV show. The survey results, showing the joint relative frequencies and marginal relative frequencies, are shown in the two-way table.

	Yes	No	Total
Children	0.3	0.4	0.7
Adults	0.25	x	0.3
Total	0.55	0.45	1

What is the value of x?

CHALLENGE AND EXTEND

The table shows the joint relative frequencies for data on how many children and teenagers attended a fair in one evening, and whether each bought a booklet of tickets for rides at the entrance gate.

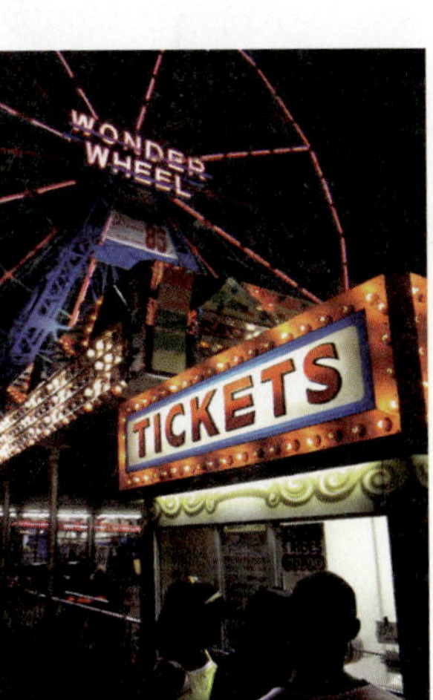

M. Scott Brauer/Alamy

	Yes	No
Children	0.125	0.1
Teenagers	0.725	0.05

Use the table to answer questions 17–20. Round answers to the nearest hundredth where appropriate.

17. Find the marginal relative frequencies for the data.

18. Based on this data, use a percentage to express how likely it is that tomorrow evening a teenager at the fair will buy a ticket booklet at the entrance. Round your answer to the nearest whole percent, if necessary.

19. If the data represent 80 teenagers and children altogether, how many children will have bought a ticket booklet at the entrance?

20. If 12 children did not buy ticket booklets at the entrance, then how many children and teenagers altogether does the data represent?

21. A poll with the options of 'yes' and 'no' was given. If the marginal relative frequency of 'yes' is 1.0, what was the marginal relative frequency of 'no'?

	Yes	No	Total
Group 1	0.24	?	?
Group 2	0.76	?	?
Total	1.0	?	?

22. **Short Response** What is the maximum a marginal relative frequency can be, and why?

SPIRAL REVIEW

Simplify each expression. *(Lesson 8-6)*

23. $\sqrt[7]{x^2}$

24. $(\sqrt{m})^6$

25. $(\sqrt[4]{y})^5$

26. $(\sqrt[8]{z^3})^8$

27. $\sqrt[3]{w^3}$

28. $\sqrt[5]{h^{45}}$

29. $\sqrt[36]{u^{12}}$

30. $\sqrt[18]{x^{36}}$

Simplify each expression, and write it by using a radical. Assume that all variables are positive.

31. $(a^2b^4)^{\frac{1}{8}}$

32. $3a^{\frac{2}{3}}(3b^2)^{\frac{1}{3}}$

For exercises 33–36, $f(x) = x^2 - 3$ and $g(x) = x + 5$. Find each function. *(Lesson 9-4)*

33. $(f + g)(x)$

34. $(f - g)(x)$

35. $(fg)(x)$

36. $\left(\frac{f}{g}\right)(x)$

Given $f(x) = 2x - 3$ and $g(x) = x^x$, find each value.

37. $f(g(1))$

38. $g(f(2))$

39. $g(f(g(2)))$

40. How many ways can you select three people for a committee out of nine candidates? *(Lesson 11-1)*

11-5A Data Gathering

Chris A. Crumley/Alamy

Objectives

Explain how random samples can be used to make inferences about a population.

Use probability to analyze decisions and strategies.

Vocabulary

population
census
sample
random sample
biased sample
statistic
parameter

Who uses this?

Researchers can use surveys to make predictions about the population of fish in a lake.

Surveys are often conducted to gather data about a population. A **population** is the entire group of people or objects that you want information about. A **census** is a survey of an entire population. When it is too difficult, expensive, or time-consuming to conduct a census, a **sample**, or part of the population, is surveyed.

When every member of a population has an equal chance of being selected for a sample, the sample is called a **random sample**, or *probability sample.* Random samples are most likely to be representative of a population and are preferred over non-random samples such as *convenience samples* and *self-selected samples.*

EXAMPLE 1 *Wildlife Application*

A wildlife researcher is studying the effects of certain pollutants on different types of fish in a lake. Because it is difficult or impossible to catch every fish in the lake, the researcher decides to use a random sample. She catches 5 groups of 10 fish each from random spots in the lake, examines them, and returns them to the lake. The table shows the numbers of perch and walleye from each group.

	Perch	Walleye
Group 1	5	5
Group 2	6	4
Group 3	3	7
Group 4	5	5
Group 5	1	9

A **Identify the population and sample in the researcher's study.**

The population is the entire group being studied, so it is the total number of fish in the lake. The sample is the 50 fish that are caught as representative of the entire population.

B **Use the table to estimate the ratio of perch to walleye in the lake.**

The sample included 20 perch and 30 walleye, so a good estimate of the ratio of perch to walleye in the lake is 2:3.

Identify the population and the sample.

1. A car factory just manufactured a load of 6,000 cars. The quality control team randomly chooses 60 cars and tests the air conditioners. They discover that 2 of the air conditioners do not work.

A non-random sample can result in a *biased sample.* A **biased sample** is a sample that may not be representative of a population. In a biased sample, the population can be underrepresented or overrepresented.

Underrepresented	One or more of the parts of a population are left out when choosing the sample.
Overrepresented	A greater emphasis is placed on one or more of the parts of a population when choosing the sample.

Random samples are less likely to be biased, while nonrandom samples are more likely to be biased. Bias in a sample is not always obvious at first glance.

EXAMPLE 2 Identifying Potentially Biased Samples

Decide whether the sampling method could result in a biased sample. Explain your reasoning.

Design Pics Inc./Alamy

 **A survey is conducted by calling 100 people randomly chosen from the phone book and asking how long each person has lived at the current residence.**

Although the sample is chosen randomly from the phone book, the people who are listed in the phone book are not necessarily representative of the entire population of the city.

In particular, anyone who recently moved may not be listed yet under his or her current number. So people who have lived in their current residence for less than a year are underrepresented. The sample is biased.

 **A survey of students at a school is conducted by contacting every 10th student from the complete roster and asking whether he or she plans to go to college.**

The sample is selected from the entire school population, and there is no group that is overrepresented or underrepresented, so the sample is not likely to be biased.

Decide whether the sampling method could result in a biased sample. Explain your reasoning.

2. An online news site asks readers to take a brief survey about whether they subscribe to a daily newspaper.

EXAMPLE 3 Analyzing a Survey

The owner of a health club wants to determine the percent of adults in his area who exercise for at least 20 minutes three times a week. He asks the first 25 adults he sees at a mall on a weekday around 10:00 A.M. Are the results of the survey likely to be representative of the population? Explain.

Do you exercise for at least 20 minutes three times a week?
Yes 32%
No 68%

The sample chosen is a convenience sample, which is not likely to be representative of the population. Also, 25 adults make up a small sample for a large population. Finally, the sample underrepresents the adults who are not at the mall on a weekday around 10:00 A.M., such as those who are at work. No, the results are not likely to be representative of the population.

3. A restaurant owner wants to know how often families in his area go out for dinner. He surveys 25 families who eat at his restaurant on Tuesday night. Are his results likely to be representative of the population? Explain.

A **statistic** is a number that describes a sample. A **parameter** is a number that describes a population. You can use a statistic from a survey to estimate a parameter. In this way, surveys can be used to make predictions about a population.

EXAMPLE 4 Making Predictions

In a survey of 50 students at a high school, 32 students said that they plan to attend the homecoming dance. The school has 720 students.

A **Which of these numbers is a statistic, and which is a parameter?**

The statistic describes the sample: 32 out of 50 students said they plan to attend the homecoming dance. The parameter describes the population. The number of students in the school that plan to attend the dance is the parameter.

B **Predict the number of students who plan to attend the homecoming dance.**

Let x be the number of students who plan to attend the dance.

$$\frac{\text{students in sample to attend}}{\text{students in sample}} = \frac{\text{students in school to attend}}{\text{students in school}}$$

$\frac{32}{50} = \frac{x}{720}$ *Substitute.*

$32 \cdot 720 = 50x$ *Cross products property*

$460.8 = x$ *Solve for x.*

You can predict that about 461 students plan to attend the dance.

4. In a random sample of phone calls to a police station, 11 of the 25 calls were for emergencies. Suppose the police station receives 175 calls in one day. Predict the number of calls that will be for emergencies.

A strong understanding of statistics is important for decision-making. An understanding of the relative importance of statistical data allows for making good, informed decisions. A poor understanding of statistics can be costly.

EXAMPLE 5 Manufacturing

Photodisc/Getty Images

A production manager conducts a product inspection of a factory that has 10 machines, each assembling 1,000 widgets per day. She hires an inspector to choose a random time in the workday and check the next 25 widgets that are made at a random machine. The inspector finds that 5 of those widgets have defects. Since 20% is too high an error rate, the manager decides to shut the factory down until the problem can be fixed. Did the manager make a good decision? Why or why not?

The manager did not make a good decision. The sample chosen was very small compared to the factory's total output, so it might not have been a representative sample. Also, because the sample was taken from only one machine, the sample was not representative of the entire factory's output.

5. A promotion on a cereal box says that 1 in 4 boxes will have a prize inside. Marion has bought 5 boxes but hasn't opened a prize. He decides the advertised prize rate must be wrong. Is he justified in this evaluation? What are the chances, to the nearest percent, of not opening a prize in 5 boxes?

THINK AND DISCUSS

1. Explain why a census cannot be biased.
2. Give an example of a parameter that can be estimated by a statistic.
3. **GET ORGANIZED** Copy and complete the graphic organizer at right. Arrange the ovals to show which terms describe the population, and which terms describe the sample.

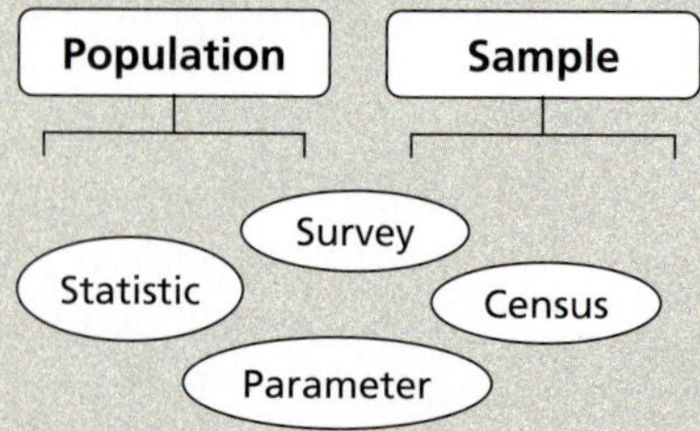

11-5A Exercises

GUIDED PRACTICE

Vocabulary **Apply the vocabulary from this lesson to answer each question.**

1. If a particular group in a population is underrepresented in a sample, the sample is ____?____. (*convenient*; *random*; *biased*)
2. A ____?____ is a measure of the population that is estimated by a statistic from a sample. (*census*; *parameter*; *survey*)

SEE EXAMPLE 1 p. CC27

Decide whether the sampling method could result in a biased sample. Explain your reasoning.

3. A survey of students at a school is taken by asking all the students that are still at the school at 5 PM whether they play sports.
4. The owner of a bakery wants to know if its customers are satisfied with its selection of baked goods. She asks the first 20 people who make a purchase on a Saturday morning.

SEE EXAMPLE 2 p. CC28

In exercises 5–7, determine whether the results of the survey are likely to be representative of the population. Explain.

The principal of a school wants to know if the students at the school would like to have wider selection of food available in the cafeteria for breakfast.

5. Survey the first 30 students who walk into the school.
6. Survey every 10th student who enters the cafeteria during the lunch period.
7. Survey every student who buys a meal in the cafeteria at least three times a week.

SEE EXAMPLE 3 p. CC29

8. In a survey of 20 sophomores at a high school, 8 students said that they would prefer a class field trip to an amusement park, rather than a museum. The sophomore class has 150 students. Predict the number of sophomores who would prefer a class trip to an amusement park.
9. In a survey of 30 employees at a company, 25 employees said that they were satisfied with their jobs. The company has 210 employees. Predict the number of employees at the company who are satisfied with their jobs.

SEE EXAMPLE 4 p. CC29

10. The manager of a radio station has a team conduct a survey about people's favorite bands. The station plays announcements at regular intervals during the day and night asking listeners to call in to the polling line and report the name of their favorite band. The team tracks the results for a week. In the report, the manager notices that 70% of his listeners name the same band as their favorite. The manager arranges for that band to play a concert to be advertised on air beforehand, in order to make a profit for the station from the ticket sales. Did the station manager make a good decision? Why or why not?
11. A chef at a restaurant that serves about 1200 customers a week introduces a dish at a special discounted price on a Wednesday night. Out of the 110 total customers that night, 45% order the dish. Because the dish sold so well, the chef decides to add it to the menu at full price. Did the chef make a good decision? Why or why not?

13. A chef at a restaurant that serves about 1200 customers a week introduces a dish at a special discounted price on a Wednesday night. Out of the 110 total customers that night, 45% order the dish. Because the dish sold so well, the chef decides to add it to the menu at full price. Did the chef make a good decision? Why or why not?

PRACTICE AND PROBLEM SOLVING

Independent Practice

For Exercises	See Example
14–15	1
16–21	2
22–25	3
27–31	4
33	5

Identify the population and the sample.

14. The manager of a department store wants to know how the shoppers at the store learned about the store's one-day sale. He asks 50 randomly chosen customers.

15. A family wants to know the average number of pieces of junk mail they receive each day. They count the pieces of junk mail that they receive each day for a week and find the average.

Decide whether the sampling method could result in a biased sample. Explain your reasoning.

16. On the first day of school, all of the incoming freshmen attend an orientation program. The principal wants to learn the opinions of the freshmen regarding the orientation program. He decides to ask the first 25 freshmen that he sees.

17. The manager of an apartment building wants to know if the residents are satisfied with his service. He writes each apartment number on a piece of paper and places the pieces of paper in a hat. Then he randomly chooses 10 apartment numbers and asks the residents of the 10 apartments about his service.

18. The members of the school drama club want to know how much students are willing to pay for a ticket to one of their productions. They decide that each member of the drama club should ask five of his or her friends what they are each willing to pay.

Ian McKinnell/Photographer's Choice/Getty Images

19. The manager of a city bus system wants to know if the people who ride the buses are satisfied with the service. She decides to post mail-in surveys on each of the city's buses.

20. A writer for a travel magazine wants to learn tourists' opinions about the nightlife in a city. She decides to visit some of the tourist attractions in the city on a Thursday morning. She plans to ask the first 50 tourists she meets for their opinions.

21. **Write About It** Administrators at your school want to know if more vegetarian items should be added to the lunch menu. They want to find out how many students are vegetarians. Give an example of one sampling method that could result in a biased sample, and one that is not likely to result in a biased sample. Explain your reasoning.

In Exercises 22–25, determine whether the results of the survey are likely to be representative of the population in the following situation. Explain.

A marching band at a school is trying to decide whether having a bake sale or a raffle during a football game will earn more money for a field trip.

22. Ask every tenth person in the cafeteria at lunch on a school day whether he or she would be more likely to buy a baked good or a raffle ticket.

23. At the next football game, ask every fifth person if he or she would be more likely to buy a baked good or a raffle ticket.

24. Survey every member of the marching band.

25. Survey every customer at an upcoming bake sale that the art club is holding.

26. **ERROR ANALYSIS** The dance team wants to find out whether the student body at their school enjoyed their last production. They decide to have the dancers from the last production go around the school and randomly survey students by asking them the question "Did you like our last production?" Explain what is wrong with this method.

One hundred students out of 800 at a school were surveyed. The results are recorded in each problem below. Predict the number of students in the population that would answer similarly.

27. Twenty-five said they attended the fall play.

28. Seventy-eight said they rode the bus to school.

29. Eighty-two said they had taken an art class as an elective.

30. Sixty-four said they were members of an extracurricular club.

31. Sixty-five said they played a sport.

32. **Estimation** In a survey of 100 students, about 32 reported that they lived within walking distance of the school. The school has 893 students. Use mental math to estimate how many students in the school are within walking distance.

33. **Critical Thinking** A town recently passed a leash law for dogs. A survey asks whether the town should designate an off-leash area where dogs can roam freely in the town park. The results of the survey are shown below.

Should Spruce Park have an off-leash area?*

Yes 92%

No 8%

*From a survey of 100 dog owners

Based on the results of the survey, the town designates the off-leash area. Was this a good decision? Explain why it was a good decision or, if not, suggest a better way to gather information to make a better decision.

DLILLC/Corbis

34. In a survey of 80 students, 25 said that they planned on attending the pep rally. The school has 550 students. Predict the number of students who plan to attend the pep rally.

   (A) 55 students

   (B) 80 students

   (C) 172 students

   (D) 378 students

35. The principal of a school wants to know if the students at the school would like to have the morning announcements posted on the school's Web site. Which sampling method is most likely to yield an accurate predication about the population?

- (F) Survey every 10th student who enters the cafeteria during the lunch period.
- (G) Survey every 20th student who enters the cafeteria during the lunch period.
- (H) Survey only the students who report that they visit the school's Web site regularly.
- (J) Survey only the students who report that they do not visit the school's Web site regularly.

CHALLENGE AND EXTEND

36. A high school is made up of 19% freshmen, 27% sophomores, 29% juniors, and 25% seniors. The editor of the school newspaper wants to survey a sample of 100 students.

- **a.** Suppose the sample includes 25 students from each class. Explain why the results may be biased.
- **b.** Suggest a way to eliminate the bias.

37. Which sample is more likely to represent the population: 100 students randomly chosen from a school with 677 students, or 100 students randomly chosen from a school with 504 students? Explain.

38. A survey was taken in your school and the results showed that 646 of 760 students had performed some type of community service in the last two months. Out of a randomly chosen group of 20 students, how many would you expect to have done some type of community service in the past two months?

39. A manufacturer of compact discs will not sell a batch of discs if 3% or more of the discs in the batch are defective. A quality control inspector finds 2 defective discs in a sample of 50 discs. The sample was randomly chosen from a lot of 1000 discs. Will the manufacturer sell this batch? Explain.

40. Find the results of a survey published in a newspaper or magazine. Do you think that the results are representative of the population? Explain.

SPIRAL REVIEW

Solve. *(Lesson 5-6)*

41. $x^2 + 8x + 9 = 0$

42. $x^2 + 6x - 3 = 0$

43. $x^2 + 4x + 2 = 0$

44. $x^2 - 8x + 1 = 0$

Evaluate. Round your answer to the nearest thousandth. *(Lesson 7-3)*

45. $\log_3 5$

46. $\log_2 7$

Find $f^{-1}(x)$. *(Lesson 9-5)*

47. $f(x) = 7x + 9$

48. $f(x) = \frac{8x - 1}{2}$

49. $f(x) = x^2 + 5$

50. $f(x) = \sqrt{2x - 3}$

11-5B Surveys, Experiments, and Observational Studies

Objectives
Focus on the commonalities and differences between surveys, experiments, and observational studies.

Vocabulary
experiment
observational study
controlled experiment
control group
treatment group
randomized comparative experiment

Plustwentyseven/Getty Images

Who uses this?
Researchers use observational studies to evaluate the effect of earphones on hearing loss. (See Example 3.)

You have already seen that a survey is one way to collect data. Although surveys are useful, different situations require different techniques for gathering data.

Individuals are people, animals, or objects that are described by data. If you collect data on the fuel efficiency of cars and trucks, the individuals are vehicles. Variables are used to describe individuals. Fuel efficiency, measured in miles per gallon, is an example of a variable.

Data Collection Methods

TERM	EXAMPLE
An **experiment** imposes a treatment on individuals to collect data on their response to the treatment.	A researcher adds acetone to gasoline to measure its effect on fuel efficiency.
An **observational study** observes individuals and measures variables without controlling the individuals or their environment in any way.	A researcher wants to find out if poor nutrition affects eyesight, but it would be unethical to deliberately subject some individuals to poor nutrition.

EXAMPLE 1 **Identifying Experiments and Observational Studies**

Explain whether each situation is an experiment or an observational study.

A **A researcher asks students the average number of hours of sleep they get per night and examines whether the amount of sleep affects students' grades.**

The researcher gathers data without controlling the individuals or applying a treatment. The situation is an example of an observational study.

B **A park employee wants to know if latex paint is more durable than non-latex paint. She paints 50 benches with latex paint, and 50 with non-latex paint.**

The employee applies a treatment (painting benches with latex paint) to some of the individuals (benches). The situation is an experiment.

1. A scientist measures the height of 20 birds' nests, and counts the number of eggs to see if there is a relationship. Is this experiment or an observational study? Explain.

For data from an experiment to be useful, the experiment must be carefully designed. In a **controlled experiment**, two groups are studied under conditions that are identical except for one variable. The effects of the treatment are determined by comparing the *control group* and the *treatment group*.

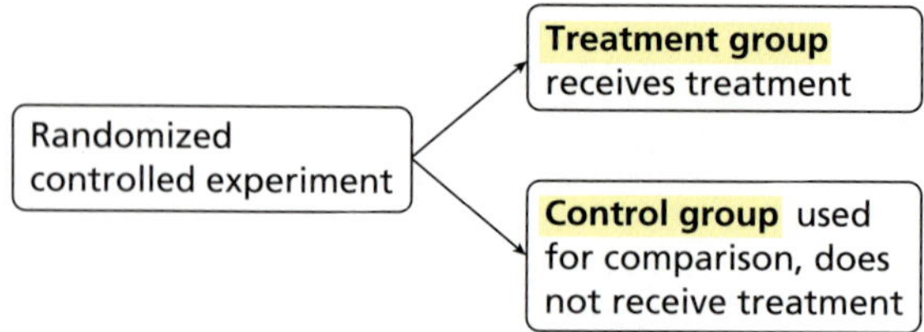

Often, to demonstrate a cause and effect hypothesis, an experiment must show two things. First, that a phenomenon occurs with the treatment; and second, that the phenomenon does not occur in the absence of the treatment.

In a **randomized comparative experiment**, the individuals are assigned to the control group or the treatment group at random, in order to minimize bias. An experiment that is not a randomized comparative experiment may be subject to bias, and any conclusions drawn from the experiment may not be valid.

EXAMPLE 2 Evaluating a Published Report

The study described in the report is a randomized comparative experiment. Describe the treatment, the treatment group, and the control group.

Milk Fights Cavities
At Ashland Middle School, fifty randomly chosen students were given milk at lunch every day for a year, and fifty other randomly chosen students were given other beverages. At the end of the year, students in the "milk" group had 15% fewer cavities than students in the other group.

The treatment in this study is *drinking milk at lunch*. The treatment group consists of the fifty students who drink milk, and the control group consists of the fifty students who were given other beverages.

2. The study described in the report is a randomized comparative experiment. Describe the treatment, the treatment group, and the control group.

A Faster Web Site
To test the redesign of its Web site, an online bookseller assembled 96 users of the site and randomly divided them into two groups. One group used the new Web site to make an online purchase and one group used the old Web site to do the same transaction. Users of the new site were able to complete the purchase 22% faster.

A randomized comparative experiment should be used to gather data whenever feasible because this type of study makes it possible to draw valid cause-and-effect conclusions.

Such experiments are also *reliable*. That is, they can be repeated and can be expected to produce similar results each time. Experiments like these are often performed in duplicate or even triplicate simultaneously.

Randomization is an important feature of experiments. When conclusions are drawn from an experiment using randomization, the results can be counted on to be useful with another, different randomized sample. If the group wasn't chosen randomly, the results would likely not be valid for any other group. Randomization of the experiment allows generalization of the results.

Generally, a controlled, randomized experiment gives the most reliable results. In some situations, however, there may be ethical or practical reasons against using an experiment. If possible, the study should still be comparative.

For example, it would be unethical to ask some individuals to smoke in order to study the effects of nicotine on their health. Therefore, an observational study should be used. To make the study comparative, the researchers should randomly choose one group of people who already smoke and one group of people who do not smoke.

EXAMPLE 3 Designing an Experiment or Observational Study

Explain whether the research topic is best addressed through an experiment or an observational study. Then explain how you would set up the experiment or the observational study.

Does listening to an MP3 player with earphones for more than one hour per day affect a person's hearing?

The treatment (listening to an MP3 player with earphones for more than one hour per day) may negatively affect an individual's hearing, so it is not ethical to assign individuals to a treatment group. Use an observational study.

Randomly choose one group of people who already listen to an MP3 player with earphones for more than one hour per day.

Randomly choose another group of people who do not listen to an MP3 player with earphones for more than one hour per day.

Monitor the hearing of the individuals in both groups at regular intervals.

Don Farrall/Getty Images

3. Explain whether the research topic is best addressed through an experiment or an observational study. Then explain how you would set up the experiment or the observational study.

Do people who consume 1000 milligrams of vitamin C each day as a dietary supplement have lower cholesterol levels than people who do not consume vitamin C supplements?

Another important feature distinguishing surveys from observational studies and experiments is that surveys are not comparative – they draw data from only one group, so they can't make conclusions about cause and effect. Well-designed studies and experiments compare data from two or more groups, allowing them to look for a relationship between variables.

It is possible to give the same survey to two or more groups and compare the results – but that is a type of observational study!

EXAMPLE 4 Evaluating Data Collection Methods

A researcher is considering three methods of evaluating two different cold medicines. Tell whether each method is a survey, an experiment or an observational study. Then explain which method would be most reliable.

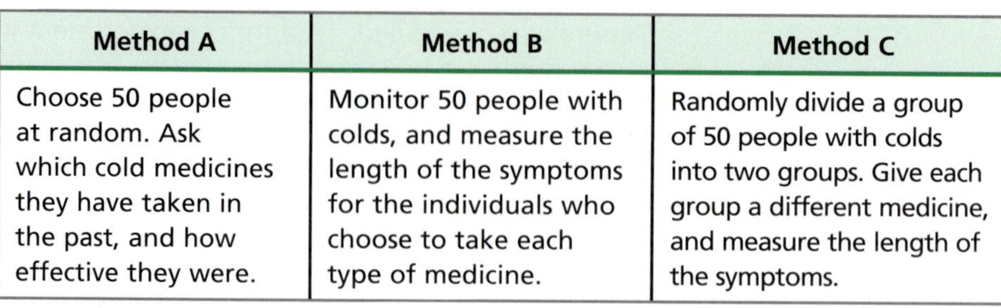

Method A	Method B	Method C
Choose 50 people at random. Ask which cold medicines they have taken in the past, and how effective they were.	Monitor 50 people with colds, and measure the length of the symptoms for the individuals who choose to take each type of medicine.	Randomly divide a group of 50 people with colds into two groups. Give each group a different medicine, and measure the length of the symptoms.

Steve Hix/Somos Images/Corbis

In method A, the researcher asks questions about cold medicines that people have taken. This method is a survey.

In method B, the researcher observes people who have chosen different cold medicines, but does not impose a treatment. This is an observational study.

In method C, the researcher gives each group a treatment, so the method is an experiment.

Method A is least reliable, because there is no basis for comparison. Method B has a comparison group, but the members are self-selected, which could lead to bias. In method C, the members of each group are randomly selected, which makes the two groups theoretically similar except for the variable, the different medicines. This method is most reliable.

4. Classify each method as a survey, an experiment, or an observational study, and explain which would be most reliable.

Method A	Method B	Method C
Randomly choose 50 people to exercise 3 hours a week, and 50 people to participate in another activity, and monitor their health.	Randomly choose 100 people. Ask how many hours a week they exercise, and how healthy they are.	Choose 50 people who exercise regularly and 50 who do not, and monitor their health.

THINK AND DISCUSS

1. Explain how an experiment is different from an observational study.

2. Describe a comparative experiment that would be considered unethical.

3. GET ORGANIZED Copy and complete the graphic organizer at right. In each column, describe the individuals in the group.

Experiment: A baker testing a new brand of yeast bakes 10 loaves with the old brand and 10 with the new brand.	
Control group:	**Treatment Group:**

11-5B Exercises

GUIDED PRACTICE

Vocabulary **Apply the vocabulary from this lesson to answer each question.**

1. A data-gathering technique that uses a treatment to influence individuals or aspects of the individuals' environment is a(n) ____?____. (*survey; observational study; experiment*)

2. Which is generally the more reliable data-gathering technique, a randomized comparative experiment or a survey?

SEE EXAMPLE 1
p. CC35

Explain whether each situation is an experiment or an observational study.

3. A caretaker at a zoo wants to study the effect of a new diet on the health of the zoo's elephants. She continues to feed half of the elephants their old food, switches the other half to a new diet, and then monitors the health of the elephants.

4. A school system wants to see if there is a correlation between students' standardized test scores and the amount of time they spend on extracurricular activities. The school board surveys students from each school in the system to gather data about the average number of hours per week spent on extracurricular activities and each student's most recent test scores.

SEE EXAMPLE 2
p. CC36

The studies described below are randomized comparative experiments. Describe the treatment, the treatment group, and the control group.

5. At Clara Barton High School, one hundred randomly chosen students were asked to stop drinking soft drinks for six months, and one hundred other randomly chosen students who were self-reported soft drink consumers were told to continue with their normal habits. At the end of six months, the students who did not drink soft drinks reported steadier energy levels throughout the school day.

6. A park service wants to determine whether reintroducing a particular species of underwater weed to their lakes would be beneficial to a particular species of fish. They plant the weed in the bed of one lake containing the species of fish. One year later, they study the health of the fish population in the lake where the weeds were reintroduced, as well as in an ecologically similar lake without the weeds.

SEE EXAMPLE 3
p. CC37

Explain whether each research topic is best addressed through an experiment or an observational study. Then explain how you would set up the experiment or the observational study.

7. Does second-hand smoke affect the health of pets?
8. Does a particular vitamin supplement make seasonal allergy symptoms less severe?
9. Does increasing the number of stoplights per mile on a road decrease the number of car accidents on the road?
10. Does a certain toothpaste prevent cavities in children better than another one?
11. Does eating chicken before playing a game of baseball increase the number of home runs scored?
12. Does eating ginger alleviate seasickness?

SEE EXAMPLE 4
p. CC38

13. A researcher is considering three methods of evaluating the effect of drinking coffee on sleep habits. Classify each method as a survey, an experiment or an observational study. Then explain which method would be most reliable.

Method A	Method B	Method C
Randomly choose 50 people to drink coffee every day. Choose another 50 people to cut all coffee out of their diet. Record the number of hours of sleep per night for each group.	Randomly choose 100 people. Ask whether they are coffee drinkers and how many hours of sleep they usually get each night.	Choose 50 people who drink coffee regularly and record how many hours of sleep they get each night. Choose another 50 who do not drink coffee, and record how many hours of sleep they get each night.

PRACTICE AND PROBLEM SOLVING

Independent Practice

For Exercises	See Example
14–18	1
19–22	2
24–29	3
31	4

Determine whether each situation is an experiment or an observational study.

14. A researcher wants to know whether babies born into homes with older siblings develop speech skills earlier than babies who are born as only children.

15. A bakery wants to know whether glaze or powdered sugar is a more enticing pastry topping. They make some pastries with each topping, and see which sells better.

16. A car dealer wants to know what color cars seem to sell the best, so she looks over the past year's sales records.

17. A cell phone manufacturer wants to investigate the user-friendliness of a new design, so the manufacturer gives the new phones to fifty people for a week and then gets their feedback.

18. A filmmaker wants to know the effect of eating fast food on his general health, so he eats fast food every day for four weeks and has doctors monitor his health.

In exercises 19–22, the study described in the report is a randomized comparative experiment. Describe the treatment, the treatment group, and the control group.

19. A pharmaceutical company wants to know about the side effects of a new blood pressure drug. Out of 200 randomly selected volunteers currently on blood pressure medication, it switches the old drug with the new drug for 100 of them, and continues to give the other 100 the old drug. It then monitors the two groups for side effects.

20. A research team wants to know whether a new laundry detergent is effective. The team washes variety of fabrics with a variety of stains in the new detergent, and washes the same pairings of fabrics and stains in just hot water, and compares the results.

21. A food company is testing a new recipe for a dinner entree. The company invites 100 people to a dinner to test the new recipe. Half the people are served the old recipe, and half are served the new recipe. They find that the people who were served the new recipe ate 15% more.

22. A battery manufacturer develops a new battery that it claims is an improvement on its existing product. A research group compares the battery life for 20 assorted devices on the new battery and the old battery, and finds that the devices run an average of 20% longer on the new battery.

23. ///ERROR ANALYSIS/// Consider the controlled experiment described below.

Mr. Johnson wants to determine what the condition of his deck would be if he did not continue to reapply wood sealant to it once every spring to protect it. So, he conducts an experiment. This spring, he uses the sealant on the entire deck except for one board. He then observes how exposure to the weather affects that board in relation to the rest of the deck.

Lindsay claims that, in the experiment, the part of the deck to which the sealant is applied corresponds to the treatment group because that is the part that is actually 'treated'. Riley claims that the single board corresponds to the treatment group. Which person is correct? Explain your reasoning.

In exercises 24–29, explain whether the research topic is best addressed through an experiment or an observational study.

24. Does using a certain brand of cleaning product put people who use it frequently at greater risk of respiratory problems?

25. Does a certain shampoo work to reduce dandruff?

26. Do people who bite their nails get sick more often than people who don't?

27. Is a certain chemical effective at killing a certain bacteria commonly found in household kitchens and bathrooms?

28. Do dogs kept as pets live longer if they run in a yard every day?

29. Does working a job for which half or more of the tasks involve typing increase the risk of certain diseases?

30. **Write About It** Explain whether the research topic below is best addressed through an experiment or an observational study. Then explain how you would set up the experiment or the observational study.

Will a car get better gas mileage if it uses Brand X motor oil?

Nicolas Loran/Getty Images

31. A researcher is considering three methods of evaluating two different brands of first aid healing ointment for minor cuts. Classify each method as a survey, an experiment or an observational study. Then explain which method would be most reliable.

Method A	Method B	Method C
Randomly divide a group of 100 people with minor cuts into two groups. Have each group use a different ointment, and record how long it takes their cuts to heal.	Choose 100 people at random. Ask which ointments they have used in the past, and how quickly their cuts have healed with each ointment.	Monitor 100 people who are currently treating minor cuts with an ointment of their choosing, and record how long it takes for them to heal.

Test Prep

32. Which of the following is generally the most reliable data-gathering technique?

(A) survey

(B) randomized comparative experiment

(C) observational study

(D) treatment

33. Which is the control group in the study described below?

> Out of a group of 100 subjects, 50 were randomly selected to receive a vitamin D supplement. All 100 subjects were monitored through the winter to see how many caught the flu.

(F) the 100 subjects randomly selected for the study

(G) subjects who caught the flu

(H) the 50 subjects who received vitamin D supplements

(J) the 50 subjects who did not receive vitamin D supplements

CHALLENGE AND EXTEND

34. Give an example of a question that could be better answered by gathering data in an observational study than it could by gathering data in an experiment. Explain why an observational study would be more appropriate. Then design an observational study that would answer the question.

35. Give an example of a question that could be better answered by gathering data in a survey than it could by gathering data in an observational study or an experiment. Explain why survey would be more appropriate. Then design a survey that would answer the question.

SPIRAL REVIEW

Solve for x. *(Lesson 5–3)*

36. $x^2 - 3x - 10 = 0$

37. $x^2 + 8x + 16 = 0$

38. $4x^2 - 9 = 0$

39. $3x^2 + 10x + 3 = 0$

Simplify the complex number expressions. *(Lesson 5–5)*

40. $(3 + 2i) - (1 - 3i)$

41. $(5 + 4i)(7 - i)$

Find the zeroes of each function.

42. $f(x) = x^2 - 11x + 32$

43. $g(x) = x^2 - 4x + 8$

44. $h(x) = 3x^2 + 8x + 6$

Find all the real values of c and d that make each equation true.

45. $3 + d + 6i = 2cd + 2di$

46. $cd + 2di = -4 - 2ci$

47. $2d + 3ci = 20 + ci + di$

For exercises 48–49 below, use the given information to find the value of x. *(Lesson 11–5)*

48. The mean of a data set is 7.4. The values in the data set are: 2, 3, 10, 15, and x.

49. The median of a data set is 73.5. The values in the data set are: 81, 62, 82, 74, 65, and x.

11-5C Significance of Experimental Results

Objective
Use simulations and hypothesis testing to compare treatments from a randomized experiment.

Vocabulary
hypothesis testing
null hypothesis

Who uses this?
Medical researchers use hypothesis testing to determine the effectiveness of new drugs. (See Example 1.)

Corbis

Suppose you flipped a coin 20 times. Even if the coin were fair, you would not necessarily get exactly 10 heads and 10 tails. But what if you got 15 heads and 5 tails, or 20 heads and no tails? You might start to think that the coin was not a fair coin, after all.

Hypothesis testing is used to determine whether the difference in two groups is likely to be caused by chance. For example, when tossing a coin 20 times, 11 heads and 9 tails is likely to occur if the coin is fair, but if you tossed 19 heads and 1 tail, you could say it was not likely to be a fair coin. To understand why, calculate the number of possible ways each result could happen. There are 2^{20} possible sequences of flips. Of these, how many fit the description '19 heads, 1 tails' and how many fit the description, '11 heads, 9 tails'?

19 heads, 1 tails	Choose 1 flip to be tails	$\binom{20}{1} = \frac{20!}{(1!)\,(19!)} = 20$
11 heads, 9 tails	Choose 9 flips to be tails	$\binom{20}{9} = \frac{20!}{(9!)\,(11!)} = 167{,}960$

Since there are $\frac{167{,}960}{20} = 8398$ times as many sequences that fit the latter description as the first, the result '11 heads, 9 tails' is 8398 times as likely as the result of '19 heads, 1 tails'! Therefore, it is very unlikely that a coin that flipped 19 heads and only 1 tails was a fair coin.

However, that outcome, while unlikely, is still possible. Hypothesis testing cannot prove that a coin is unfair – it is still possible for a coin to come up with 19 heads by chance, it is just very unlikely. Therefore, you can only say how likely or unlikely a coin is to be biased.

Hypothesis testing begins with an assumption called the *null hypothesis*. The **null hypothesis** states that there is no difference between the two groups being tested. The purpose of hypothesis testing is to use experimental data to test the viability of the null hypothesis.

Helpful Hint
The word *null* means "zero," so the *null* hypothesis is that the difference between the two groups is zero.

The null hypothesis is often the reverse of what the experimenter believes; it is presented to allow the data to contradict it.

For a coin toss, the null hypothesis is that coin is *not* biased: the number of heads will equal the number of tails. The null hypothesis is *rejected* if the difference is too large, which in this case means that it is likely that the coin is not fair.

In a randomized controlled experiment, the null hypothesis is that there is no difference in the value of the variable for the control group and treatment group.

EXAMPLE 1 Analyzing a Controlled Experiment

A medical researcher is testing a new gel coating for a pill, and wants to know if it affects absorption. In a random trial, blood samples were taken from 12 patients in each group 30 minutes after ingesting the pill. The drug levels in micrograms per milliliter are shown below.

Control group	41	43	43	42	36	39	44	50	40	40	34	47
Treatment group	34	26	33	27	37	29	39	33	24	34	37	31

A **State the null hypothesis for the experiment.**

The null hypothesis is that the blood levels of the drug will be the same for the control group and the treatment group.

B **Compare the results for the control group and the treatment group. Do you think that the researcher has enough evidence to reject the null hypothesis?**

You can use box-and-whisker plots to compare the results for the control group and the treatment group.

First, arrange the data in order and find the median, quartiles, minimum, and maximum. Then draw a box-and-whisker plot for each group.

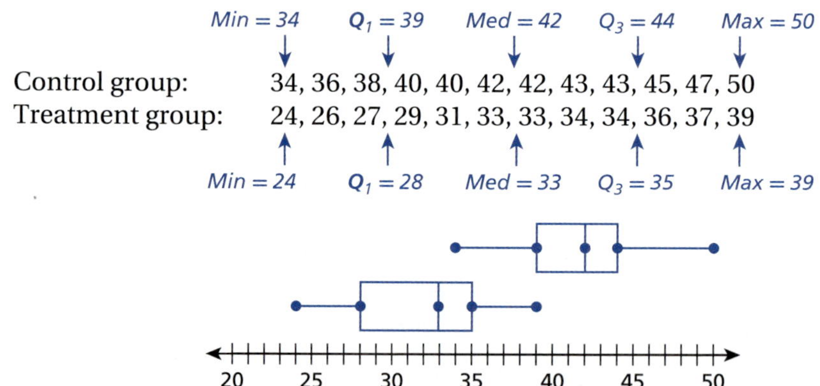

There is a large difference in the two groups that is unlikely to be caused by chance. The researcher should reject the null hypothesis, which means that the coating probably does affect absorption.

1. A teacher wants to know if students in her morning class do better on a test than students in her afternoon class. She compares the test scores of 10 randomly chosen students in each class.

Morning class: 76, 81, 71, 80, 88, 66, 79, 67, 85, 68
Afternoon class: 80, 91, 74, 92, 80, 80, 88, 67, 75, 78

a. State the null hypothesis.

b. Compare the results of the two groups. Does the teacher have enough evidence to reject the null hypothesis?

Hypothesis testing can be used to compare the mean from a sample to the mean of a population. If the sample contains at least 30 individuals, you can use the *z-test*. Suppose that the population mean is estimated to be μ, and a random sample has n individuals ($n \geq 30$). To find the z-value of a statistic, you need to know the sample mean $\overline{x}$ and standard deviation σ. The *z-value* is found using the following formula:

$$z = \frac{\overline{x} - \mu}{\frac{\sigma}{\sqrt{n}}}$$

The null hypothesis is that there is no difference in the two groups. If the sample mean is close to the population mean, then the z-value is close to 0. If the z-value is too large, you can reject the null hypothesis.

One common measure used in z-tests is known as a 95% confidence level:

- If $|z| > 1.96$, then you can reject the null hypothesis with 95% certainty.
- If $|z| < 1.96$, then you do not have enough evidence to reject the null hypothesis.

EXAMPLE 2

Using a *z*-Test

A test prep company claims it can boost SAT scores to an average of 1800. In a random sample of 36 students who took the course, the average was 1745, with a standard deviation of 210. Is there enough evidence to reject the claim?

Greg Hinsdale/Corbis

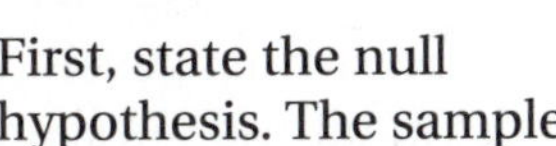

First, state the null hypothesis. The sample mean is 1745, and the company claims that the population mean is 1800. The null hypothesis is that there is no difference in the sample and the population.

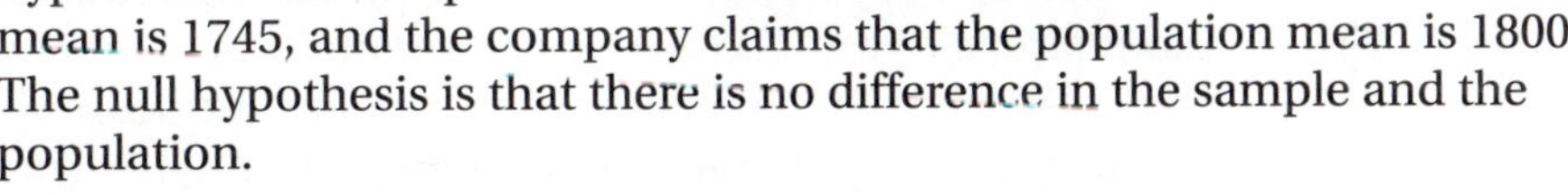

Next, find the z-value, using $\mu = 1800$, $\overline{x} = 1745$, $\sigma = 210$, and $n = 36$.

$$z = \frac{\overline{x} - \mu}{\frac{\sigma}{\sqrt{n}}}$$

$$z = \frac{1745 - 1800}{\frac{210}{\sqrt{36}}} = \frac{-55}{35} \approx -1.57$$

Because $|z| = 1.57 < 1.96$, you do not have enough evidence to reject the claim with 95% confidence. This does not necessarily mean that the claim is true, just that you cannot prove it is false.

2. A tax preparer claims an average refund of \$3000. In a random sample of 40 clients, the average refund was \$2600, and the standard deviation was \$300. Is there enough evidence to reject his claim?

THINK AND DISCUSS

1. Give an example of a null hypothesis.
2. Explain what is true if you do not reject the null hypothesis.
3. **GET ORGANIZED** Copy and complete the graphic organizer at right. Arrange the steps of the z-test in the correct order.

If $|z| < 1.96$, do not reject the null hypothesis.

State the null hypothesis.

If $|z| > 1.96$, reject the null hypothesis.

Find the z-value.

11-5C Exercises

GUIDED PRACTICE

Vocabulary **Apply the vocabulary from this lesson to answer each question.**

1. If a difference between the treatment group and the control group in a randomized controlled experiment is caused by __?__, the z-value will be close to 0. (*chance*; *experimental error*)

2. The __?__ in randomized controlled experiment is that there is no difference between the treatment group and the control group. (*conclusion*; *null hypothesis*)

Use the following information to complete exercises 3–4.

A labor union is testing whether a professional development program in a certain industry has been successful in raising the scores of new employees on a standardized test. The given tables contain data for each of two companies in the industry. The data for each company show the scores of the new employees who have undergone the professional development program (the treatment group) and the scores of those who have not (the control group).

SEE EXAMPLE 1 p. CC44

3. The data for Company A is shown below.

Control group	82	77	82	78	90	72	80	87	70	68	88	85
Treatment group	92	84	88	95	89	84	79	85	94	90	85	92

   a. State the null hypothesis for the experiment.
   b. Compare the results for the control group and the treatment group. Do you think that the researcher has enough evidence to reject the null hypothesis?

4. The data for Company B is shown below.

Control group	77	89	75	91	68	82	80	89	74	78	83	80
Treatment group	88	87	79	82	90	87	92	85	84	88	94	76

   a. State the null hypothesis for the experiment.
   b. Compare the results for the control group and the treatment group. Do you think that the researcher has enough evidence to reject the null hypothesis?

SEE EXAMPLE 2
p. CC45

5. **Investment** An investment consultation firm claims that it will increase the returns on its clients' investments to an average of 20% of the original investments, with minimal risk involved. In a random sample of 50 clients of the firm, the average return on investments with minimal risk was 18.5% of the original investment, with a standard deviation of 4%. What is the z-value rounded to the nearest hundredth, and is there enough evidence to reject the firm's claim?

6. The publishers of a study guide claim that their book will increase average quarterly math grades of users to 85%. In a random sample of 20 students who have used the study guide, the math grade was 88%, with a standard deviation of 8%. What is the z-value rounded to the nearest hundredth, and is there enough evidence to reject the publishers' claim?

PRACTICE AND PROBLEM SOLVING

Independent Practice

For Exercises	See Example
7–9	1
10–13	2

7. **Water Quality** A city is conducting a water quality study. It is measuring trace levels of a certain substance in the blood of residents who live in a city with unknown water quality against the same substance in another city with water quality that is known to be high. The blood levels of the substance in micrograms per milliliter are shown in the chart.

Known quality	9	5	4	7	5	8	7	3	4	6	8	5
Unknown quality	2	4	8	5	9	7	9	5	4	10	5	2

a. State the null hypothesis for the experiment.

b. Compare the results for the control group and the treatment group. Do you think that the researcher has enough evidence to reject the null hypothesis?

Use the following information to complete exercises 8–9 below.

Botany A researcher is investigating the health of some plants that have been treated with a chemical to increase their rate of growth. In the problems below, there are data given about levels of two different elements in the plants. The data for each element show the levels of the element in the treated plants, and the levels of the element in untreated plants.

8. The nitrogen levels of the treated and untreated plants are given in parts per million in the chart below.

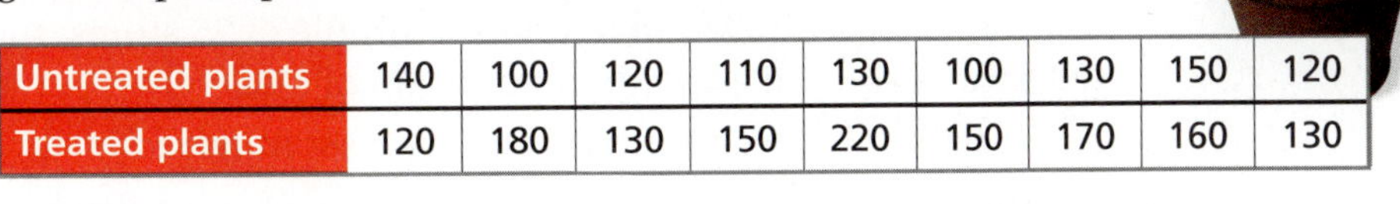

Untreated plants	140	100	120	110	130	100	130	150	120
Treated plants	120	180	130	150	220	150	170	160	130

a. State the null hypothesis about nitrogen for the experiment.

b. Compare the results for the control group and the treatment group. Do you think that the researcher has enough evidence to reject the null hypothesis?

9. The potassium levels of the treated and untreated plants are given in parts per million in the chart below.

Untreated plants	200	250	320	310	340	310	270	340	370
Treated plants	310	260	280	310	220	260	290	220	250

a. State the null hypothesis about potassium for the experiment.

b. Compare the results for the control group and the treatment group. Do you think that the researcher has enough evidence to reject the null hypothesis?

10. **Medicine** A pharmaceutical company has developed a new drug to treat high blood pressure. Blood pressure measures are given as two distinct numbers, known as the systolic and diastolic pressures, both measured in millimeters of mercury (mm Hg). The company claims that the drug will decrease systolic pressure to an average of 120 mm Hg, and diastolic to an average of 80 mm Hg.

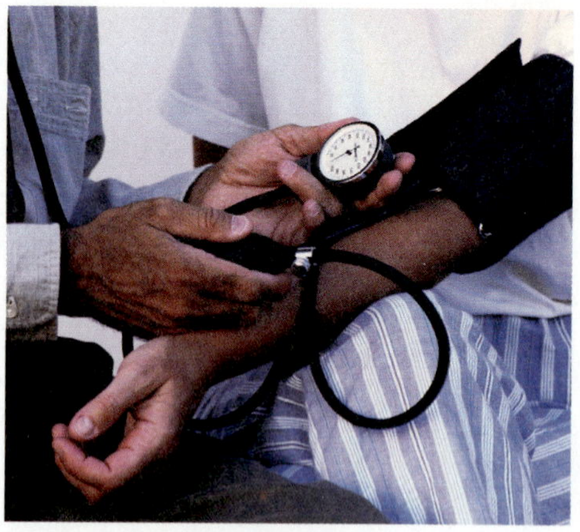
Photodisc/Getty Images

An independent trial is conducted by treating a random sample of 20 people with the drug. The findings are presented in the chart. Find the z-scores for the two trials, rounded to the nearest hundredth, and choose whether or not to reject the company's claims.

Company's Claims	Avg. systolic 120 mm Hg	Avg. diastolic 80 mm Hg
Trial results	Avg. 122 mm Hg	Avg. 85 mm Hg
Standard Dev.	10 mm Hg	8 mm Hg
z-score	a. ________	c. ________
Reject claim?	b. Yes / No	d. Yes / No

11. A math teacher claimed that the average grade of the students in her Algebra 2 classes this year would be equal to the average grade of the same students in Algebra 1 classes last year. The average grade of last year's Algebra 1 students was a 92%. In a random sample of 25 current Algebra 2 students, the average grade was 87%, with a standard deviation of 7%.
    a. Find the z-value, rounded to the nearest hundredth.
    b. Is there enough evidence to reject the teacher's claim?

12. A car insurance company claims that it will save new customers 15% of what they pay for their current plans with other companies. In a random sample of 30 new customers, the average amount saved was 8% with a standard deviation of 2%.
    a. Find the z-value, rounded to the nearest hundredth.
    b. Is there enough evidence to reject the insurance company's claim?

13. **Marketing** A marketing firm claims that its ad campaign will increase sales for a fast-food chain by 15%. In a random sample of 25 stores, the average increase in sales was 14% with a standard deviation of 5%.
    a. Find the z-value, rounded to the nearest hundredth.
    b. Is there enough evidence to reject the marketing firm's claim?

14. **Write About It** Translate the formula for calculating z-values into English instructions.

15. **Critical Thinking** Consider the two statements below:
    I. This drug raises insulin levels in the blood stream.
    II. It will rain tomorrow.

    Which of these claims is a candidate for hypothesis testing? Can each statement be proven either true or false with certainty today? Explain.

16. **Critical Thinking** What does a positive z-value indicate about the values of the mean in the entire population versus the value of the mean in the sample? What does a negative z-value indicate about the same two values?

17. ///ERROR ANALYSIS/// A claim is made that the mean of a data set will be 60. In a test of the claim, the mean among 16 trials is actually 58, with a standard deviation of 3. Shondell rejects the claim based on her calculation of the *z*-value, but Mandy says rejection is unjustified based on her calculation of the *z*-value. Whose work is correct? Explain the error.

Shondell's work	Mandy's work
$Z = \frac{58 - 60}{\frac{3}{\sqrt{16}}}$	$Z = \frac{58 - 60}{\frac{3}{\sqrt{16}}}$
$Z = \frac{58 - 60}{\frac{3}{4}}$	$Z = \frac{58 - 60}{\frac{3}{4}}$
$Z = \frac{-2}{\left(\frac{3}{4}\right)}$	$Z = \frac{-2}{\left(\frac{3}{4}\right)}$
$Z = -2 \times \frac{4}{3}$	$Z = -2 \times \frac{3}{4}$
$Z = -\frac{8}{3}$	$Z = -\frac{6}{4}$
$Z \approx -2.67$	$Z \approx -1.5$

TEST PREP

18. Which measure is not needed for calculating a *z*-value, given data about a treatment group and a control group?

Ⓐ standard deviation for the population

Ⓑ standard deviation for the sample

Ⓒ mean of the population

Ⓓ mean of the sample

19. A claim is made that the mean of a data set will be 4.7. In a test of the claim, the mean among 49 trials is actually 5, with a standard deviation of 0.5. Which is the *z*-value of the given data, rounded to the nearest hundredth?

Ⓕ 11.67   Ⓗ 4.20

Ⓖ 1.96   Ⓙ 0.021

CHALLENGE AND EXTEND

20. A foreign language teacher wants to know whether strength of math skills is a good indicator of how a student will do in a foreign language. The class average among the students with average math skills is 87.6%. The teacher records the test scores of 5 students in her class with particularly strong math skills separately. The results are shown in the table.

Strong math student scores	89	78	90	85	92

a. Find the mean and the standard deviation of the scores, rounded to the nearest percentage point, for the students with strong math skills.

b. State the null hypothesis for the teacher's experiment.

c. Find a *z*-value, rounded to the nearest hundredth, and use it to evaluate the null hypothesis.

21. **ERROR ANALYSIS** Thaddeus and Billy are analyzing the results of an experiment in science class. Their science teacher tells them they should expect to see a mean value of 54 in their data, if the experiment is performed correctly. After 15 trials, the mean value they actually measure is 50, with a standard deviation of 5. Thaddeus' and Billy's claims are presented below. Whose logic is correct, assuming the teacher is right about the expected results? Justify your answer.

Thaddeus	Billy
The mean we measured was far off from what was expected, so we can be sure that we performed the experiment incorrectly.	"It can't be proved that our results fall outside the expected range. It's possible that we got these results while performing the experiment correctly."

SPIRAL REVIEW

Graph the function. *(Lesson 5-1)*

22. $f(x) = x^2 + 2$

23. $f(x) = (x{-}1)^2$

Match each graph with one of the following functions.

A. $a(x) = -2x^2 + 5x$

B. $b(x) = 3(x - 4)^2 - 2$

C. $c(x) = 3(x - 2)^2 - 2$

24.

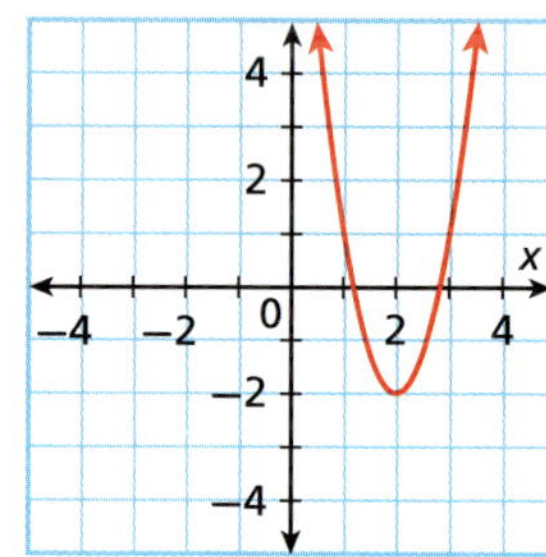

25.

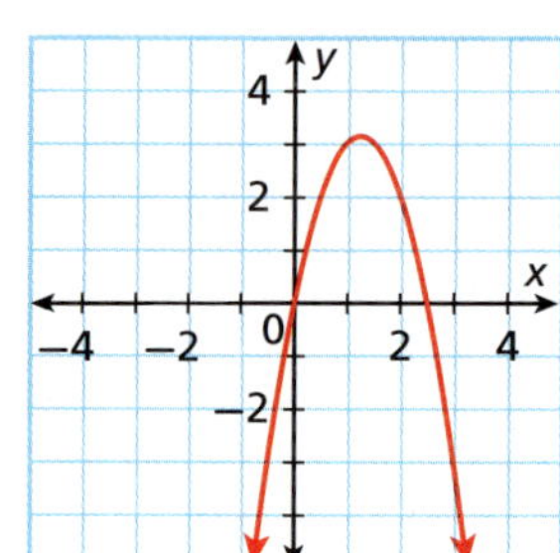

26.

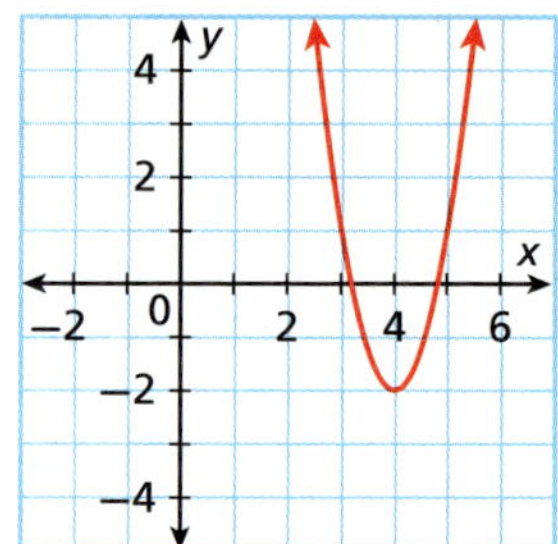

Solve for *x*. *(Lesson 7-6)*

27. $\ln e^{x+6} = 7$

28. $e^{\ln 5x} = 30$

29. Four coins are flipped. What is the probability that all will land on heads? *(Lesson 11-2)*

30. Which is the more likely sequence of eight coin flips: H, T, T, H, T, H, T, T or H, H, H, H, H, H, H, H? Explain.

31. Two integers from 15 to 24 (inclusive) are randomly selected. The same number can be chosen twice. What is the probability both numbers are greater than 20?

32. Two integers from 15 to 24 (inclusive) are randomly selected. The same number cannot be chosen twice. What is the probability both numbers are greater than 20?

11-5D Sampling Distributions

Objective
Estimate population means and proportions and develop margin of error from simulations involving random sampling.

Analyze surveys, experiments, and observational studies to judge the validity of the conclusion.

Vocabulary
simple random sample
systematic sample
stratified sample
cluster sample
convenience sample
self-selected sample
probability sample
margin of error

Who uses this?
Pollsters use different survey methods to accurately reflect public opinion.

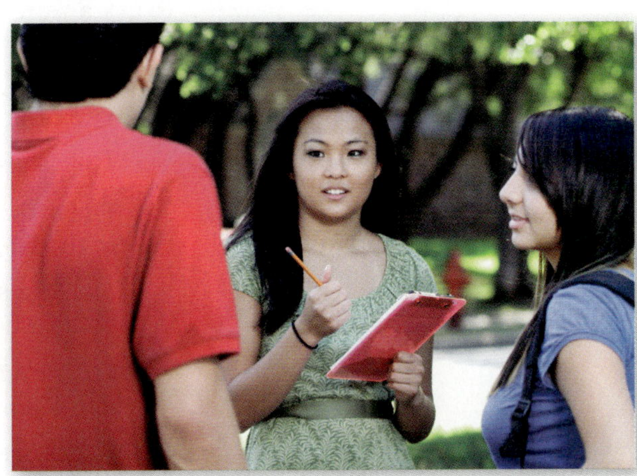

When a survey is used to gather data, it is important to consider how the sample is selected for the survey. If the sampling method is biased, the survey will not accurately reflect the population.

Most national polls that are reported in the news are conducted using careful sampling methods in order to minimize bias. Other polls, such as those where people phone in to express their opinion, are not usually reliable as a reflection of the general population.

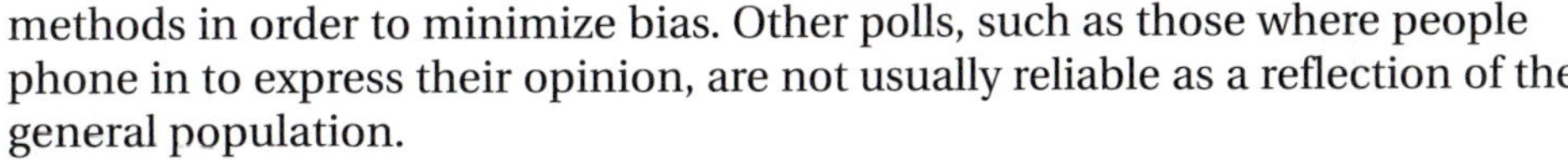

Remember that a random sample is one that involves chance. Six different types of samples are shown below.

Types of Samples

Simple Random Sample
Members are chosen using a method that gives everyone an equally likely chance of being selected.

Systematic Sample
Members are chosen using a pattern, such as selecting every other person.

Stratified Sample
The population is first divided into groups. Then members are randomly chosen from each group.

Cluster Sample
The population is first divided into groups. A sample of the groups is randomly chosen. All members of the chosen groups are surveyed.

Convenience Sample
Members are chosen because they are easily accessible.

Self-Selected Sample
Members volunteer to participate.

EXAMPLE 1 Classifying a Sample

Comstock/Getty Images

The officials of the National Football League (NFL) want to know how the players feel about some proposed changes to the NFL rules. They decide to ask a sample of about 100 players. Classify each sample.

A **The officials choose the first 100 players who volunteer their opinions.**

This is a self-selected sample because the players volunteer.

B **The officials randomly choose 3 players from each of the 32 teams in the NFL.**

This is a stratified sample because the players are separated by team and randomly chosen from each team.

C **The officials have a computer generate a list of 100 players from a database that includes all of the players in the NFL.**

This is a simple random sample because each player has an equally likely chance of being chosen.

CHECK IT OUT!

1. The editor of a snowboarding magazine wants to know the readers' favorite places to snowboard. The latest issue of the magazine included a survey, and 238 readers completed and returned the survey. Classify the sample.

When choosing a sampling method, the most important concerns are usually accuracy and budget. The most accurate survey is a census, because it samples every individual in the population. However, a census is not always possible.

The sampling methods that are more accurate tend to be more difficult or expensive. For example, if you wanted a simple random sample of the entire United States, you would need a list of every person in the country to choose from.

A **probability sample** is a sample where every member of the population being sampled has a nonzero probability of being selected. Simple random samples, stratified samples, and cluster samples are all examples of probability sampling. However, not every sampling method performed is a probability sample. A convenience sampling is not a probability sample, because people in the population who are not convenient for the surveyor to survey have no chance of being surveyed.

Self-selected sampling is also not a probability sample, although the reason why is more subtle. This kind of sampling is not a probability sample because the members of the population that don't self-select have no chance of being surveyed.

These non-probability methods of sampling are usually the easiest to conduct, but also the least reliable.

Most Accurate	Very Accurate	Not Very Accurate
census	simple random sample stratified sample cluster sample	convenience sample self-selected sample

EXAMPLE 2

Evaluating Sampling Methods

A high school has 552 freshmen, 495 sophomores, 449 juniors, and 439 seniors enrolled. The student newspaper wants to take a survey of the school. Classify each sampling method. Which is most accurate? Which is least accurate? Explain your reasoning.

Method A Randomly select 50 freshmen, 50 sophomores, 50 juniors, and 50 seniors from the complete roster.

Method B Randomly select 200 students from the complete roster.

Method C Choose every 10th student who enters the cafeteria at lunchtime.

Method A is a stratified sample. The population is divided into groups, and a sample is randomly selected from each group. Method B is a simple random sample, and Method C is a convenience sample.

Method B is the most accurate, because every member of the population is equally likely to be in the sample. In Method A, the sample contains an equal number of freshmen and seniors, even though there are 552 freshmen and 439 seniors in the population. So seniors are overrepresented in the sample.

Method C is the least accurate, because some individuals may not have a chance of being included, such as those who do not eat in the cafeteria.

2. A small-town newspaper wants to report on public opinion about the new City Hall building. Classify each sampling method. Which is most accurate? Which is least accurate? Explain your reasoning.

Method A Ask readers to write in and give their opinion.

Method B Survey 10 randomly selected female students and 10 randomly selected male students in the cafeteria during the lunch period.

Method C Randomly choose 10 streets in the town and survey everyone who lives on each street.

Imagine a polling organization that surveys 1000 voters in a city to find out how they plan to vote in an upcoming mayoral election. The organization reports that 58% of city residents plan to vote for Smith, and that the survey has a *margin of error* of ±3%. The margin of error expresses the amount of error in the survey results due to the nature of random sampling.

The **margin of error** of a random sample defines an interval, centered on the sample percent, in which the population percent is most likely to lie. In the above example, the margin of error of ±3% means that the percent of voters in the population who plan to vote for Smith is likely to lie within 3 percentage points of 58%. That is, it is likely that between 55% and 61% of city voters plan to vote for Smith.

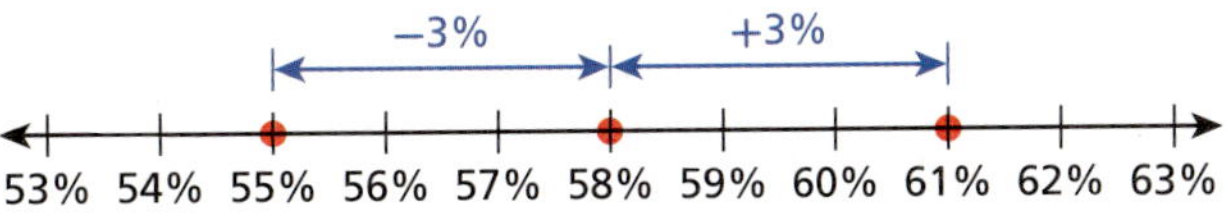

EXAMPLE 3 Interpreting a Margin of Error

Students at a high school will vote on a proposal to start classes later in the day. According to a survey of a random sample of students, 54% of the students agree with the proposal and 46% of the students disagree with the proposal. The survey's margin of error is ±5%. Does the survey clearly project the outcome of the voting?

Use the margin of error to find an interval in which the actual percent of students who agree with the proposal is likely to lie.

54% ± 5% represents the interval 54% – 5% = 49% to 54% + 5% = 59%.

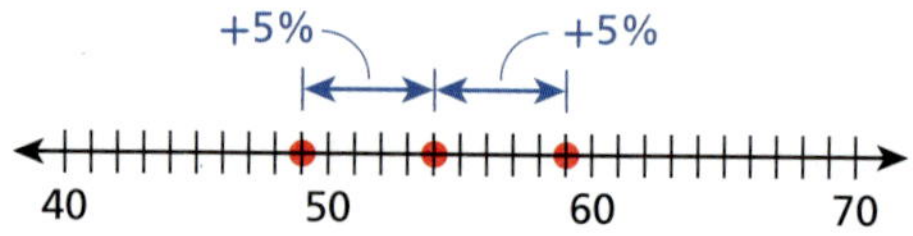

Use the margin of error to find an interval in which the actual percent of students who disagree with the proposal is likely to lie.

46% ± 5% represents the interval 46% – 5% = 41% to 46% + 5% = 51%.

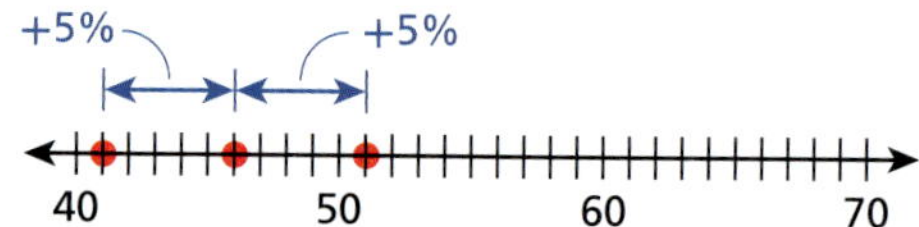

You can conclude that between 49% and 59% of all students agree with the proposal and between 41% and 51% of all students disagree with the proposal. Because the intervals overlap, the survey does not clearly project the outcome of the voting.

3. A survey of a random sample of voters shows that 38% of voters plan to vote for Gonzalez, 31% of voters plan to vote for Chang, and 31% plan to vote for Harris. The survey has a margin of error of ±3%. Does the survey clearly project the outcome of the voting? Explain.

THINK AND DISCUSS

1. Explain the difference between a stratified sample and a cluster sample.
2. Describe how to find the interval that is likely to contain the actual percent of voters who favor a proposition, if a survey result is 63% and the margin of error is ±3%.
3. **GET ORGANIZED** Copy and complete the graphic organizer below. In each oval, write a sampling method.

11-5D Exercises

GUIDED PRACTICE

1. **Vocabulary** Add and subtract the ____?____ from the reported percentage of people in favor of one response to find the interval in which the actual percentage lies. (*standard deviation; margin of error*)

SEE EXAMPLE 1
p. CC52

Classify each sample.

2. **Radio** The host of a radio show wants to know the listeners' favorite bands. He asks listeners to call the radio station and tell him their favorite bands.

3. **Customer Satisfaction** The owner of a lawn care company wants to know if his clients are satisfied with the company's service. He decides to ask 15 clients, randomly chosen from a list of his 32 clients, for their opinions of the company's service.

4. **Business** The general manager of a fast-food restaurant chain wants to determine the interest in a new food item that he is considering adding to the menu in the next month. He has the local manager at each of the 10 restaurants in the chain survey 20 randomly selected people throughout the day.

SEE EXAMPLE 2
p. CC53

5. **School Administration** A high school has 228 freshmen, 309 sophomores, 322 juniors, and 260 seniors enrolled. The principal of a school wants to know whether the students at the school would like to have a print-making class or a computer repair class offered as a spring elective. Classify each sampling method. Which is most accurate? Which is least accurate? Explain your reasoning.

   Method A Randomly choose 80 students who enter the cafeteria during the lunch period.

   Method B Randomly choose 20 freshmen, 20 sophomores, 20 juniors, and 20 seniors from the cafeteria during lunch period.

   Method C Survey every sophomore and senior.

For exercises 6–7, determine whether the survey clearly projects the winner. Explain your response.

SEE EXAMPLE 3
p. CC54

6. **Student Government** According to a survey of a random sample of students voting for student council president, 57% planned to vote for James and 43% plan to vote for Thea. The survey's margin of error is ±6%.

7. **Elections** A community association surveys its members about who they'd like to have as the next chairman, Hickory or Washington. In the survey, 36% preferred Hickory and 64% preferred Washington. The survey's margin of error is ±9%.

PRACTICE AND PROBLEM SOLVING

Independent Practice

For Exercises	See Example
8–15	1
17, 18	2
20, 21	3

Classify each sample.

8. **Television** The programming director of a local television station decides to conduct a survey to find out if the station's viewers prefer to watch the local news at 5:30 or 6:00. He asks each viewer to call a toll-free number and state his or her preference.

9. **Business** The manager of a credit union wants to know whether its members utilize the online services offered on the credit union's Web site. He randomly selects 20 members registered as local patrons of each at the five branches of the credit union to call and ask whether they use the online services.

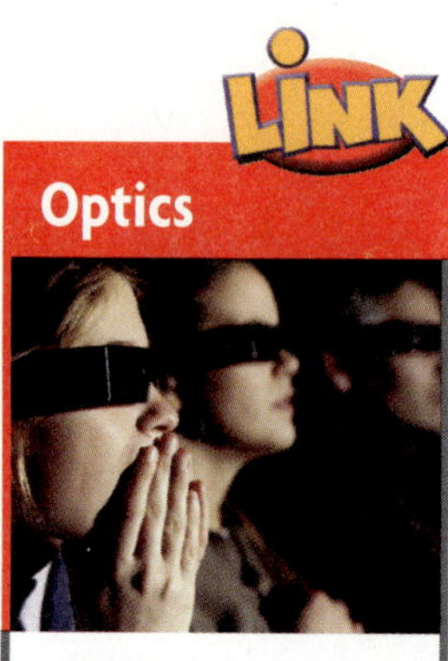

Optics

3D movies are shown by projecting two slightly different images on the screen. Each image is polarized, and each lens of the glasses permits only light that is polarized a certain way. In this way, the glasses control which of the two projections each eye is seeing, which your eyes combine to form a 3D image.

10. **Local Government** Town officials are deciding whether to build a public parking lot downtown. The officials decide to ask residents to come to a town hall meeting to participate in a vote on the issue.

11. **Human Resources** The human resources manager at a business wants to know how satisfied the company's employees are with their jobs. She surveys the 20 people who sit closest to her office.

12. **Scientific Research** The researchers at a hearing research center want to know if the music played during aerobics classes at health clubs is loud enough to cause hearing damage.They randomly choose 10 health clubs from the 150 health clubs in the area and measure the loudness of the music played during the aerobics classes.

13. **Customer Satisfaction** The manager of a movie theater wants to know how the movie viewers feel about the new 3D glasses at the theater. She asks every 30th person who exits the theater each Saturday night for a month.

14. **Journalism** A writer for a travel magazine wants to learn tourists' opinions about the nightlife in a city. She decides to visit a different tourist attraction every day for a week. She will have the magazine's interns, who are traveling with her, interview every tourist they see at each attraction.

15. **Student Government** Your class officers are planning a dance, and they want to know if they should hire a disc jockey or a live band. They decide to survey every tenth student as he or she leaves at the end of the school day.

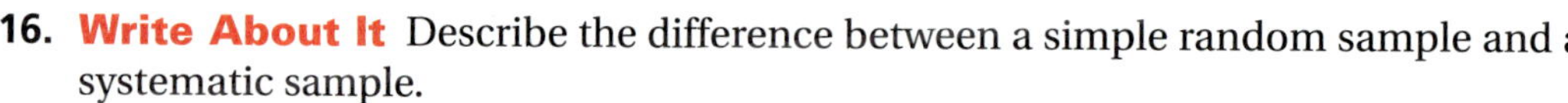

16. **Write About It** Describe the difference between a simple random sample and a systematic sample.

17. **School Administration** A principal wants to know how teachers feel about changes to their schedule. He decides to ask a sample of 20 teachers. Classify each sampling method. Which is most accurate? Which is least accurate?

    Method A Randomly choose 2 teachers from each of the school's 10 departments of various sizes.

    Method B Survey the first 20 teachers who volunteer.

    Method C Randomly choose 20 teachers from an alphabetical list of the 60 teachers in the school.

18. **Quality Control** The manager of the produce department at a grocery store receives ten crates of oranges. She wants to examine the shipment to determine the quality of the fruit. Classify each sampling method. Which is most accurate? Which is least accurate?

    Method A Open the first crate and examine the fruit on the top.

    Method B Examine every fruit in a third of the crates.

    Method C Examine several randomly selected oranges from each of the ten crates.

19. **Critical Thinking** The editor of a school newspaper wants to survey students about which one of the following methods of communication they prefer: talking on the telephone, writing e-mail, or using text messaging.

a. Describe a sampling method that can be used so that the sample will best represent the population.

b. Write a question to ask the members of the sample.

20. **Local Government** Town officials in Lauraville want to build a new fire station on Northern Avenue. A local newspaper surveys residents about the new fire station. The results are shown below.

Should the new fire station be on Northern Avenue?

Yes 56%
No 44%

Margin of error: ±4%

Does the survey clearly show the majority's preference? Explain your response.

21. **Student Government** The sophomore class student council conducted a survey to determine whether the sophomore class would prefer a class trip to an amusement park or a museum. Among students surveyed, 55% preferred the museum and 45% preferred the amusement park. The survey's margin of error is ±6%. Does the survey clearly indicate the majority's preference? Explain your response.

22. **///ERROR ANALYSIS///** A reporter for a school newspaper surveys a random sample of students to find out for whom they plan to vote in an upcoming election for student body president. The survey's results are shown below.

Diedrich	58%
LeBlanc	42%

Margin of error: ±12%

Diedrich begins to celebrate his win based on the results of the survey. LeBlanc chides him and tells him not to be so sure he'll win in the actual election because even the survey is inconclusive. Who has a more accurate understanding of the results? Explain.

23. The manager of a clothing store wants to know whether shoppers are satisfied with the store's products. She sends a survey to shoppers who signed up to be on the store's mailing list. Which type of sample is she gathering?

(A) convenience

(B) self-selected

(C) simple random

(D) systematic

24. Every registered voter in Humboldt County receives a questionnaire in the mail they can fill out and return. What type of sample is this?

(A) convenience
(B) self-selected
(C) simple random
(D) systematic

25. Which of the following sampling types is not a probability sample?

(A) stratified
(B) cluster
(C) simple random
(D) convenience

26. Which tends to be the most reliable sampling technique?

(F) stratified
(G) self-selected
(H) simple random
(J) convenience

CHALLENGE AND EXTEND

27. **Local Government** City officials want to conduct a survey about an upcoming election. Describe how to generate a simple random sample, a systematic sample, and a stratified sample of the registered voters in the city.

28. **Medical Research** A medical conference has 500 participating doctors. The table lists the doctors' specialties. A researcher wants to survey a sample of 25 of the doctors to get their opinions on a new medical device.

Specialty	Number of Doctors
Dermatology	40
Oncology	140
Surgery	100
Geriatrics	120
Pediatrics	100

a. Explain why it may be better for the researcher to use a stratified sample rather than a simple random sample.

b. When a stratified sample is chosen using *proportionate allocation*, the size of each group in the sample is proportional to the size of the group in the population. Assuming the researcher uses proportionate allocation, how many dermatologists should be in the sample?

29. **ERROR ANALYSIS** Identify which of the following survey questions are likely to result in a biased sample. For each one you identify, revise the question to remove the tendency toward bias.

a. Do you favor the proposal to increase spending on technology in our schools?

b. Do you like the refreshing taste of sample A or the flat taste of sample B?

c. Would you rather read a boring book or watch an exciting movie?

d. Do you, like most people your age, enjoy watching music videos?

SPIRAL REVIEW

Name the degree and leading coefficient of the polynomial. Then name the polynomial according to how many terms it has. *(Lesson 6-1)*

30. $5x^2 + 9x + 2$

31. $6xy^5$

Describe how y varies with x in each: directly, inversely, or jointly. *(Lesson 8-1)*

32. $y = \frac{5}{x}$

33. $y = \frac{1}{3}x$

34. Two integers between 1 and 20 are chosen at random. The same number can be chosen twice. What is the probability that both numbers are multiples of 3? *(Lesson 11-2)*

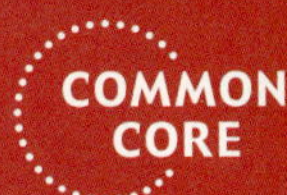

Mastering the Standards

for Mathematical Practice

The topics described in the Standards for Mathematical Content will vary from year to year. However, the *way* in which you learn, study, and think about mathematics will not. The Standards for Mathematical Practice describe skills that you will use in all of your math courses.

Mathematical Practices

1. *Make sense of problems and persevere in solving them.*
2. *Reason abstractly and quantitatively.*
3. *Construct viable arguments and critique the reasoning of others.*
4. *Model with mathematics.*
5. *Use appropriate tools strategically.*
6. *Attend to precision.*
7. *Look for and make use of structure.*
8. *Look for and express regularity in repeated reasoning.*

4 Model with mathematics.

Mathematically proficient students can apply... mathematics... to... problems... in everyday life, society, and the workplace...

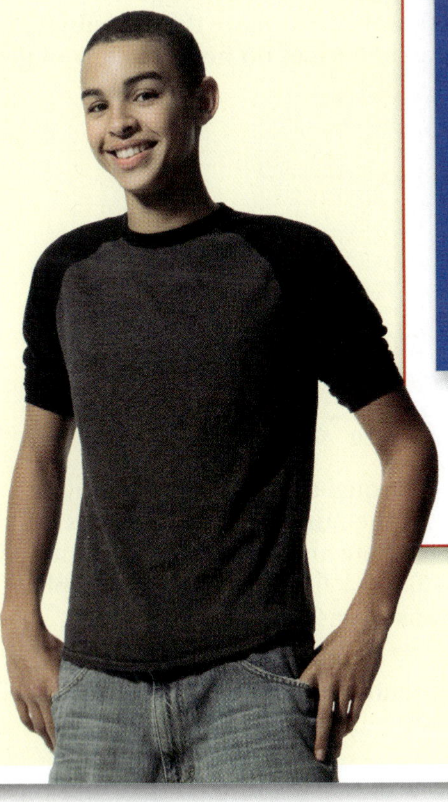

PhotoDisc/Getty Images

In your book

Multi-Step Test Prep and **Real-World Connections** apply mathematics to other disciplines and in real-world scenarios.

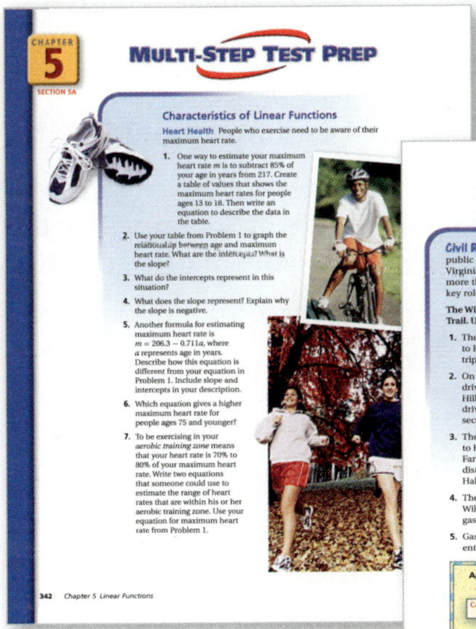

CHAPTER 5
SECTION 5A

MULTI-STEP TEST PREP

Characteristics of Linear Functions

Heart Health People who exercise need to be aware of their maximum heart rate.

1. One way to estimate your maximum heart rate m is to subtract 85% of your age in years from 217. Create a table of values that shows the maximum heart rates for people ages 13 to 18. Then write an equation to describe the data in the table.
2. Use your table from Problem 1 to graph the relationship between age and maximum heart rate. What are the intercepts? What is the slope?
3. What do the intercepts represent in this situation?
4. What does the slope represent? Explain why the slope is negative.
5. Another formula for estimating maximum heart rate is $m = 206.3 - 0.711a$, where a represents age in years. Describe how this equation is different from your equation in Problem 1. Include slope and intercepts in your description.
6. Which equation gives a higher maximum heart rate for people ages 75 and younger?
7. To be exercising in your *aerobic training zone* means that your heart rate is 70% to 80% of your maximum heart rate. Write two equations that someone could use to estimate the range of heart rates that are within his or her aerobic training zone. Use your equation for maximum heart rate from Problem 1.

342 *Chapter 5 Linear Functions*

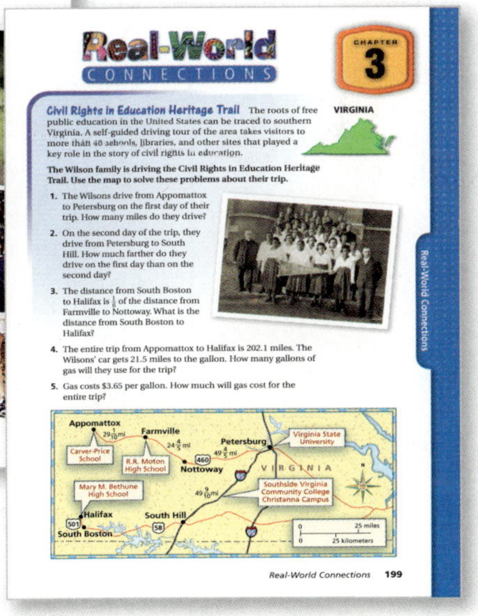

Real-World CONNECTIONS

CHAPTER 3

Civil Rights in Education Heritage Trail The roots of free public education in the United States can be traced to southern Virginia. A self-guided driving tour of the area takes visitors to more than 40 schools, libraries, and other sites that played a key role in the story of civil rights in education.

VIRGINIA

The Wilson family is driving the Civil Rights in Education Heritage Trail. Use the map to solve these problems about their trip.

1. The Wilsons drive from Appomattox to Petersburg on the first day of their trip. How many miles do they drive?
2. On the second day of the trip, they drive from Petersburg to South Hill. How much farther do they drive on the first day than on the second day?
3. The distance from South Boston to Halifax is $\frac{1}{6}$ of the distance from Farmville to Nottoway. What is the distance from South Boston to Halifax?
4. The entire trip from Appomattox to Halifax is 202.1 miles. The Wilsons' car gets 21.5 miles to the gallon. How many gallons of gas will they use for the trip?
5. Gas costs $3.65 per gallon. How much will gas cost for the entire trip?

Real-World Connections

Real-World Connections 199

11-6A Fitting to a Normal Distribution

Objectives
Use tables to estimate areas under normal curves.

Recognize data sets that are not normal.

Vocabulary
standard normal value

Who uses this?
Biologists can use standard normal values to study animal populations. (See Example 3.)

Normal curves are used in a wide variety of situations to estimate probabilities. Remember that the maximum value of the curve occurs at the mean, and that the curve is symmetric about a vertical line through the mean. If a random variable x has a mean of μ, and standard deviation of σ, then nearly all of the area under the curve (99.7%) is within three standard deviations from the mean (between $\mu - 3\sigma$ and $\mu + 3\sigma$).

The total area under a normal curve is always 1. The area under the curve between two x-values corresponds to the probability that x is between those values.

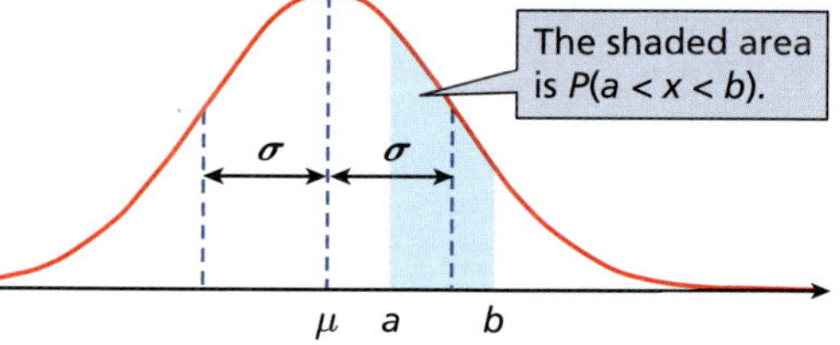

EXAMPLE 1 Finding Joint and Marginal Relative Frequencies

Jamie can drive her car an average of 432 gallons per tank of gas, with a standard deviation of 36 miles. Use the graph to estimate the probability that Jamie will be able to drive more than 450 miles on her next tank of gas.

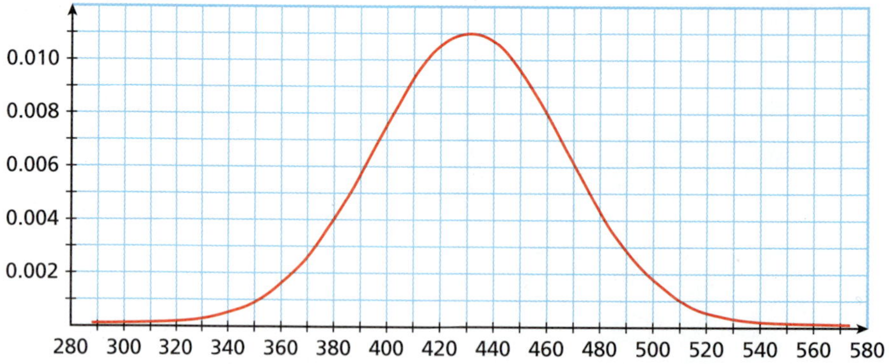

The area under the normal curve is always equal to 1. Each square on the grid has an area of $10(0.001) = 0.01$. Count the number of grid squares under the curve for values of x greater than 450. There are about 31 squares under the graph, so the probability is about $31(0.01) = 0.31$ that she will be able to drive more than 450 miles on her next tank of gas.

1. Using the graph above, estimate the probability that Jamie will be able to drive less than 400 miles on her next tank of gas.

All normal curves have the same basic shape. If μ is changed, the curve shifts left or right. If σ is changed, the curve is stretched vertically and compressed vertically, or vice versa. The *standard normal curve* has a mean of $\mu = 0$ and standard deviation of $\sigma = 1$, and is found by adjusting the variable in question, x, to match the standard normal curve.

Standard Normal Values

If a random variable x is normally distributed with mean μ and standard deviation σ, then the **standard normal value** of x is given by the following formula:

$$z = \frac{x - \mu}{\sigma}$$

The area under the normal curve between $x = a$ and $x = b$ is equal to the area between the standard normal values of a and b.

The table shows the approximate area under the standard normal curve for all values less than z for selected values of z.

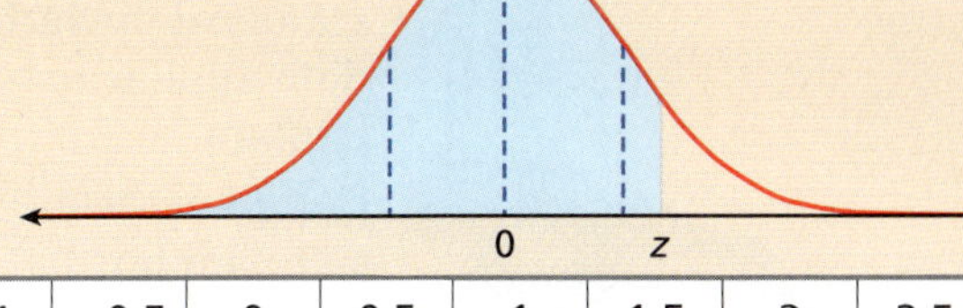

z	−2.5	−2	−1.5	−1	−0.5	0	0.5	1	1.5	2	2.5
Area	0.01	0.02	0.07	0.16	0.31	0.5	0.69	0.84	0.93	0.98	0.99

EXAMPLE 2 Using Standard Normal Values

Scores on a test are normally distributed with a mean of 75 and a standard deviation of 8.

 Estimate the probability that a randomly selected student scored less than 87.

First, find the standard normal value of 87, using $\mu = 75$ and $\sigma = 8$.

$$z = \frac{x - \mu}{\sigma} = \frac{87 - 75}{8} = \frac{12}{8} = 1.5$$

Use the table to find the area under the curve for all values less than 1.5, which is 0.93. The probability of scoring less than 87 is about 0.93.

 Estimate the probability that a randomly selected student scored between 71 and 75.

Find the standard normal values of 71 and 75. Use the table to find the areas under the curve for all values less than z.

$$z = \frac{71 - 75}{8} = \frac{-4}{8} = -0.5 \quad \text{Area} \approx 0.31 \qquad z = \frac{75 - 75}{8} = 0 \quad \text{Area} = 0.5$$

Subtract the areas to eliminate where the regions overlap. The probability of scoring between 71 and 75 is about $0.5 - 0.31 = 0.19$.

2. Scores on a test are normally distributed with a mean of 142 and a standard deviation of 18. Estimate the probability of scoring above 106.

There are many data sets in a variety of situations that can be modeled by using a normal curve. However, not all data is normally distributed. Sometimes the "tail" is longer on one side than the other, resulting in a skewed distribution.

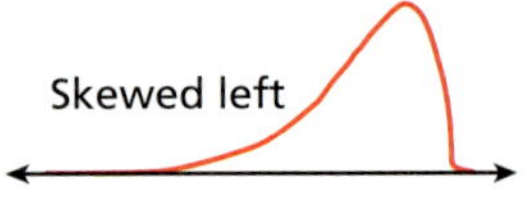

You can compare the data to the areas under the curve to determine whether the normal curve is a good fit for a data set. For example, about half of the values should be less than the mean.

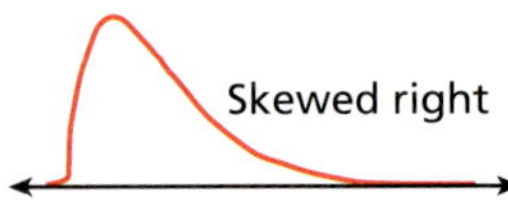

EXAMPLE 3 Determining Whether Data May Be Normally Distributed

A biologist is measuring the lengths of frogs in a certain location. The lengths of 20 frogs randomly chosen from the sample are shown. If the mean is 7.4 cm and the standard deviation is 0.8 cm, does the data appear to be normally distributed? Explain.

Length (cm)				
7.6	5.8	7.9	7.6	8.1
7.9	7.1	5.9	8.4	7.3
7.1	6.4	8.3	8.4	6.7
8.2	7.8	5.9	6.8	8.1

Compare the areas under the standard normal curve to the number of data values.

The projected number of values that corresponds to each value of z is close to the actual number of data values. The data appears to be normally distributed.

z	Area below z	x	Values below x	
			Projected	Actual
−2	0.02	5.8	0	0
−1	0.16	6.6	3	4
0	0.5	7.4	10	9
1	0.84	8.2	17	17
2	0.98	9	20	20

3. A random sample of salaries at a company is shown. If the mean is \$37,000 and the standard deviation is \$16,000, does the data appear to be normally distributed?

Salaries (thousands \$)					
61	33	29	28	32	43
29	35	34	22	64	35
32	25	28	29	25	84

THINK AND DISCUSS

1. Explain how to find the standard normal value of the random variable x if the mean is 50 and the standard deviation is 5.
2. Describe the relationship between the areas under the normal curve for all x-values less than a and for all x-values greater than a.
3. **GET ORGANIZED** Copy the normal curve at right. Write the area in each section of the graph.

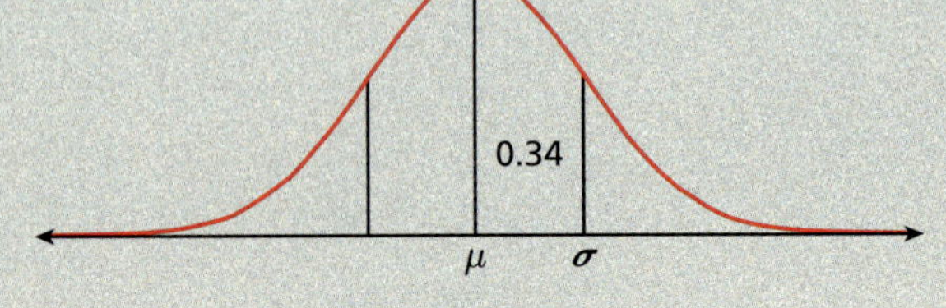

11-6A Exercises

GUIDED PRACTICE

1. **Vocabulary** How is the *standard normal value* of a statistic related to the mean and standard deviation of the random variable?

SEE EXAMPLE 1
p. CC60

2. In Ms. Bartholomew's class, the average amount of time spent studying for the test was 7.5 hours, with a standard deviation of 1.6 hours. Use the graph to estimate the probability that a randomly selected student spent more than 6 hours studying for the test.

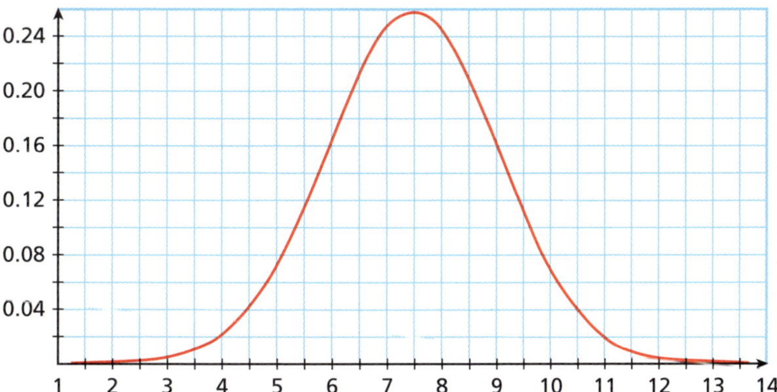

SEE EXAMPLE 2
p. CC61

Scores on a test are normally distributed with a mean of 70 and a standard deviation of 10. For questions 3–6, use the table below to find each probability.

z	−2.5	−2	−1.5	−1	−0.5	0	0.5	1	1.5	2	2.5
Area	0.01	0.02	0.07	0.16	0.31	0.5	0.69	0.84	0.93	0.98	0.99

3. A randomly selected student scored below 65.
4. A randomly selected student scored above 80.
5. A randomly selected student scored between 50 and 60.
6. A randomly selected student scored between 70 and 90.

SEE EXAMPLE 3
p. CC62

7. The weights of a sample of 30 potatoes from a farm are given below. If the mean is 0.5 lb and the standard deviation is 0.1 lb, does the data appear to be normally distributed? Explain.

0.55	0.45	0.50	0.44	0.61
0.45	0.49	0.53	0.75	0.49
0.44	0.46	0.35	0.45	0.48
0.66	0.33	0.60	0.49	0.66
0.41	0.52	0.58	0.41	0.64
0.39	0.54	0.48	0.57	0.43

PRACTICE AND PROBLEM SOLVING

Independent Practice	
For Exercises	See Example
8	1
9–12	2
13	3

8. At a bottling plant, the amount of liquid in 12-ounce bottles is normally distributed with a mean of 12 ounces and a standard deviation of 0.15 ounces. If an inspector chooses a bottle at random, use the graph to estimate the probability that it will contain between 11.9 and 12.1 ounces.

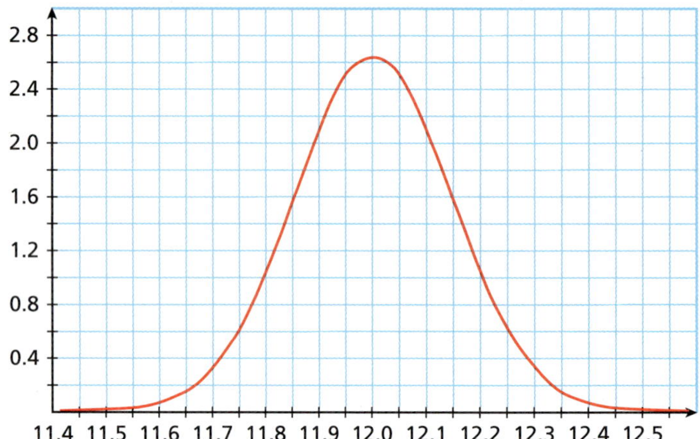

Scores on a test are normally distributed with a mean of 76 and a standard deviation of 6. For questions 9–12, use the table below to find each probability.

z	−2.5	−2	−1.5	−1	−0.5	0	0.5	1	1.5	2	2.5
Area	0.01	0.02	0.07	0.16	0.31	0.5	0.69	0.84	0.93	0.98	0.99

9. A randomly selected student scored below 64.

10. A randomly selected student scored above 70.

11. A randomly selected student scored between 85 and 91.

12. A randomly selected student scored between 73 and 79.

13. The heights of 24 children on a merry-go-round in a park are given below. If the mean of all the children at the park is 45 inches and the standard deviation is 6 inches, does the data appear to be normally distributed? Explain.

50	44	51	52	53	51	51	48
53	53	46	51	45	54	48	51
47	50	45	48	46	52	50	52

Greg Balfour Evans/Alamy

For a normally distributed random variable x with $\mu = 100$ and $\sigma = 16$, find each probability.

14. $x > 100$

15. $x < 140$

16. $92 < x < 108$

17. $x < 84$

18. $60 < x < 124$

19. $x < 68$ or $x > 132$

20. **Write About It** Apples at an orchard are packaged in approximately 5-lb bags. Each bag contains a whole number of apples. The weights are normally distributed with a mean of 5 lb and a standard deviation of 0.25 lb. An inspector weighs each bag, and rejects all bags that weigh less than 5 lb. Describe the shape of the distribution of the weights of the bags that are not rejected.

TEST PREP

21. If x is a normally distributed random variable with mean μ and standard deviation σ, then what is the probability that $x < \mu$?

    Ⓐ 0.16 Ⓒ 0.84

    Ⓑ 0.5 Ⓓ 0.99

22. Scores on a test are normally distributed with a mean of 78 and a standard deviation of 6. A student is selected at random. Which has the greatest probability?

    Ⓕ The student's score is greater than 90.

    Ⓖ The student's score is less than 69.

    Ⓗ The student's score is between 78 and 81.

    Ⓙ The student's score is between 63 and 72.

CHALLENGE AND EXTEND

Suppose that x is a normally distributed random variable with mean μ and standard deviation σ.

23. If $\mu = 65$ and $P(x > 70) = 0.31$, what is σ?

24. If $\sigma = 12$ and $P(x < 30) = 0.07$, what is μ?

25. If $P(x < 16) = 0.16$ and $P(x > 26) = 0.93$, what are μ and σ?

26. **Critical Thinking** Suppose that $f(x)$ is the equation of a normal curve with mean μ and standard deviation σ.

    a. What is the effect of the transformation $f(x - \mu)$?

    b. What is the effect of the transformation $f\left(\frac{x}{\sigma}\right)$?

    c. If $z = \frac{x - \mu}{\sigma}$, describe the relationship of $f(x)$ and $f(z)$.

SPIRAL REVIEW

Evaluate. *(Lesson 11-1)*

27. ${}_{12}P_4$ 28. ${}_{12}P_8$ 29. ${}_{12}C_4$ 30. ${}_{12}C_8$

There are 2 yellow and 6 red marbles in a bag. Find the probability of each of the following. *(Lesson 11-2)*

31. The chosen marble is red.

32. The chosen marble is green.

A bag contains 4 red tiles with the letters A, B, C, and D, 4 blue tiles with the letters E, F, G, and H, and 4 yellow tiles with the letters I, J, K, and L. Find each probability. *(Lesson 11-4)*

33. choosing a red tile or a vowel

34. choosing a yellow or blue tile

35. choosing a letter in the word *and*

36. choosing a blue tile with a consonant

11-6B Analyzing Decisions

Brand X Pictures/Getty Images

Objectives
Explain that probability can be used to help determine if good decisions are made. Use probabilities to analyze decisions and strategies.

Who uses this?
Insurance policies use the probability of certain outcomes to calculate the premiums they will charge individuals. The individuals who examine the data are called actuaries.

In experiments with numerical outcomes, the **expected value (EV)** is the weighted average of the numerical outcomes of a probability experiment. To find the expected value of an event, multiply each possible outcome of the event by the likelihood of that outcome. The expected value of an event with k potential outcomes $n_1, n_2, n_3, \ldots n_k$ each with probability $p_1, p_2, p_3 \ldots p_k$ is given by $EV = n_1p_1 + n_2p_2 + n_3p_3 + \ldots + n_kp_k$.

Probability

The probabiity *P* of an event *A* can be found by using

$$P(A) = \frac{\text{number of ways even occurs}}{\text{total number of outcomes}}$$

In addition, when conducting an experiment, the sum of the probabilities is equal to 1.

That is, for an experiment with events *A*, *B*, *C*, and *D* in an experiment,

$$P(A) + P(B) + P(C) + P(D) = 1$$

EXAMPLE 1 **Finding Expected Value**

A **What is the expected value of a six-sided number cube with sides labeled 1–6?**

The probability for each number is listed in the table below.

Value of Side	1	2	3	4	5	6
Probability	$\frac{1}{6}$	$\frac{1}{6}$	$\frac{1}{6}$	$\frac{1}{6}$	$\frac{1}{6}$	$\frac{1}{6}$

$$EV = 1\left(\frac{1}{6}\right) + 2\left(\frac{1}{6}\right) + 3\left(\frac{1}{6}\right) + 4\left(\frac{1}{6}\right) + 5\left(\frac{1}{6}\right) + 6\left(\frac{1}{6}\right)$$

$$EV = \frac{1+2+3+4+5+6}{6} = \frac{21}{6} = 3.5$$

Notice that the expected value of rolling the cube (3.5) is *not* one of the possible outcomes.

B **What is the expected value of the sum of rolling two six-sided number cubes with sides labeled 1 through 6?**

Let $EV(X)$ represent the expected value of the first number cube and $EV(Y)$ represent the expected value of the second number cube.

$EV(X + Y) = EV(X) + EV(Y)$

Since both number cubes are labeled in the same way, use the information from part A to solve:

$EV(X) = 3.5$ and $EV(Y) = 3.5$

So, $EV(X) + EV(Y) = 7$.

The expected value of rolling two six-sided number cubes is 7.

1. What is the expected value of rolling the six-sided number cube as shown in the net below?

Expected value can be used to make decisions in business, insurance settings, traffic, games, and other situations. For example, if two people want to end a game early, they can use the expected value to verify who was the most likely to win.

EXAMPLE 2 Using Expected Value in Real-World Situations

Lisa has two choices of route when she goes to school. Route A always takes 15 minutes. Route B takes 12 minutes, unless there is a traffic jam, in which case that route will take 20 minutes. If the chance of a traffic jam is 15%, which route should she take?

To find the best route, compare the expected value for each route.

$EV(A) = 1(15) = 15$ minutes

$EV(B) = 0.15(20) + 0.85(12) = 3 + 10.2 = 13.2$ minutes

Since the expected value for Route B is lower than the estimated value of Route A, Lisa should take Route B.

2. Jack can take one of three routes to work each day. Route A takes 16 minutes, Route B takes 10 minutes, and Route C takes 20 minutes. There is a 40% chance he will encounter an accident in Route A, which increases travel time to 25 minutes. There is also a 20% chance he will encounter a traffic jam if he takes Route B, which increases his travel time to 40 minutes. He has a 10% chance of experiencing a delay in Route C, which increases his travel time to 32 minutes. Which route should Jack take to work each day?

EXAMPLE 3

The Monty Hall Problem

The Monty Hall problem is a problem derived from a TV game show. On the show, the contestant is challenged to choose from one of the three closed doors.

Two of the doors hide goats, while the third door hides a prize. Once the contestant picks a door, the host, who knows the contents behind each door, opens one of the other doors to reveal a goat. If both remaining doors contain a goat, the host chooses randomly which door to reveal. The host then offers the contestant a chance to stay with their original choice of door or switch his choice to the other remaining door. What should the contestant do?

The Monty Hall problem is a tricky problem. Many assume changing doors either does not matter or that each door has the same probability of containing the prize. They reason that since there is one prize and two doors, there is a 50% chance each of the two remaining doors will contain the prize. But that is incorrect! Let's examine at all the possibilities.

Assume the contestant picks door A initially.

Contents Behind Each Door			Results	
Door A	Door B	Door C	Result if door is switched	Result if door is not switched
Car	Goat	Goat	Goat	Car
Goat	Car	Goat	Car	Goat
Goat	Goat	Car	Car	Goat

Notice that if the contestant switches doors, they have a $\frac{2}{3}$ chance of winning the prize while they only have a $\frac{1}{3}$ chance of winning the car if they keep the door they initially chose. The expected value of switching is twice that of staying with the original choice!

If you were in the game show, would you switch doors?

3. Mikayla is applying to 3 colleges. She makes estimates of her chances of being accepted, and estimates of her chances of receiving financial aid from each, presented below:

	% chance of acceptance	% chance of financial aid
College A	75%	30%
College B	65%	40%
College C	70%	45%

At which college is she most likely to be both accepted and receive financial aid?

Expected Value

In an experiment with k events, n_k represents the value of each individual event, and $P(n_k)$ represents the probability of n_k.

Outcome	1	2	...	k
Value	n_1	n_2	...	n_k
Probability	$P(n_1)$	$P(n_2)$	...	$P(n_k)$
	$n_1P(n_1)$	$n_2P(n_2)$		$n_kP(n_k)$

The expected value is

$$EV = n_1P(n_1) + n_2P(n_2) + \cdots + n_kP(n_k)$$

THINK AND DISCUSS

1. Explain how the expected value in an experiment is different from the individual probabilities.
2. Give an example of a situation where you could use expected value in your everyday life. Describe how you could use expected value to help you make a decision.
3. **GET ORGANIZED** Copy and complete the graphic organizer. Use the table to find the expected value of the experiment with the given probability distribution.

Outcome	A	B	C	
Value	10	5	1	
Probability	0.05	0.2	0.75	Expected Value

11-6B Exercises

GUIDED PRACTICE

1. **Vocabulary** The weighted average of the outcomes in an experiment is its ___?___ (*expected value* or *probability*).

SEE EXAMPLE 1
p. CC66

Find the expected value for each of the number cubes with the given sides.

2.

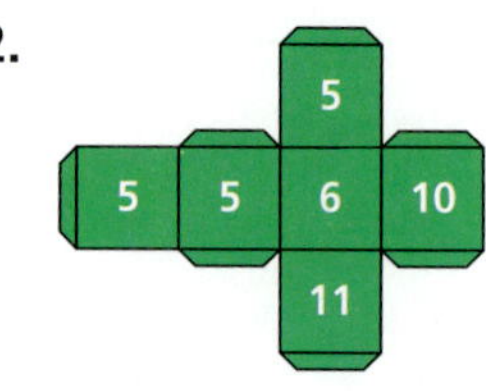

3.

4
2 12 3 8
4

4.

1
1 1 1 1
10

5. Find the expected value for the sum of the number cubes in exercises 2 and 3.

SEE EXAMPLE 2
p. CC67

6. Gloria can take two routes to get to work. Route A takes 14 minutes without traffic, but 25 minutes with traffic. Route B takes 10 minutes without traffic, and 30 minutes with traffic. She estimates a 20% chance of encountering traffic on Route A and a 40% chance of encountering traffic on Route B. Which route would you recommend Gloria take? Explain.

SEE EXAMPLE 3
p. CC68

7. In a game show, a contestant must choose a question from one of three categories. Questions in category A are worth $500, but there is a penalty of $100 for each incorrect answer. Questions in category B are worth $100, with a $20 penalty for incorrect answers. Questions in category C are worth $50, with no penalty for incorrect answers. The probability of answering correctly is 0.1 for category A, 0.3 for category B, and 0.6 for category C. Which category has the highest expected value?

PRACTICE AND PROBLEM SOLVING

Independent Practice

For Exercises	See Example
8–11	1
12–13	2
23	3

Find the expected value for each of the number cubes with the given sides.

8.

2
1 2 4 10
9

9.

10.

11. Find the expected value for the sum of the number cubes in exercises 9 and 10.

12. Tristan is buying a new camera, and is deciding whether to purchase a 1-year warranty. The warranty costs $50, and covers all repairs. If he does not get the warranty, then within the first year he estimates there is a 5% chance he will have to replace the camera for $180, and a 15% chance that he will need a repair costing $60. Should he buy the warranty? Explain.

CreativeAct-Technology series/Alamy

13. A high school is having a raffle to raise funds. The top prize is worth $2,000 and the probability of winning is 0.1%. The second prize is worth $150 and the probability of winning is 2%. Using expected value, find the expected value of a raffle ticket.

Find the expected value for each of the spinners shown.

14.

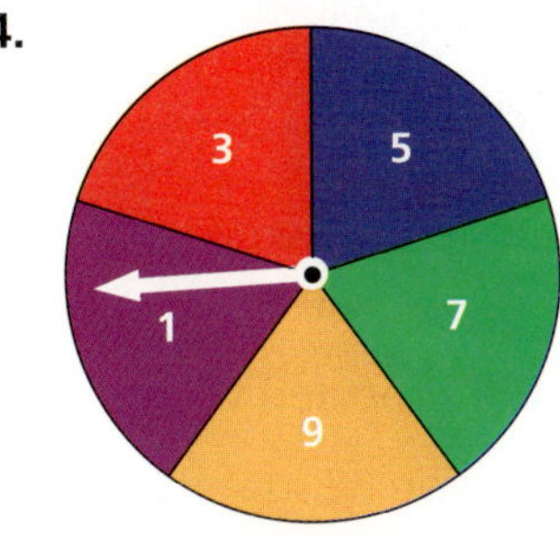

15.

16.

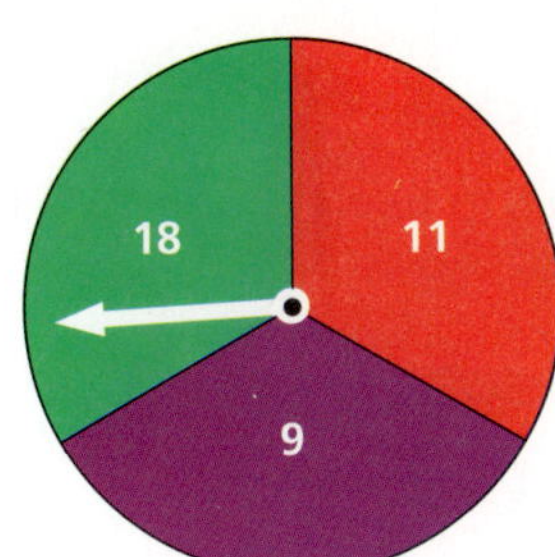

17.

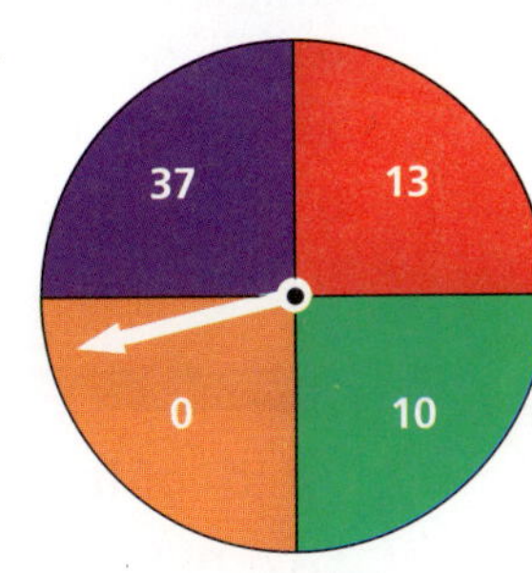

Find the expected value for each of the unequal spinners shown.

18.

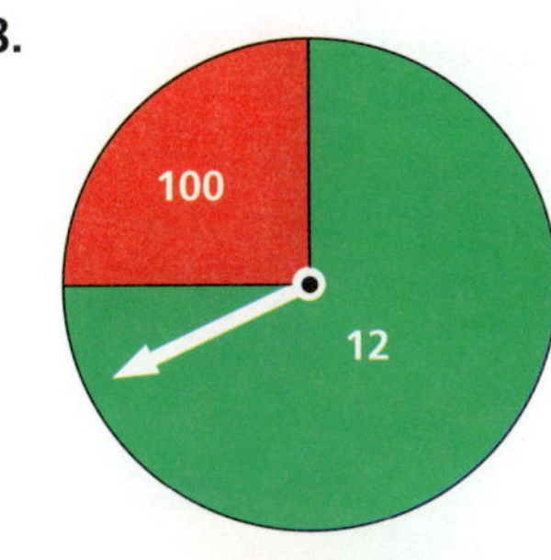

19.

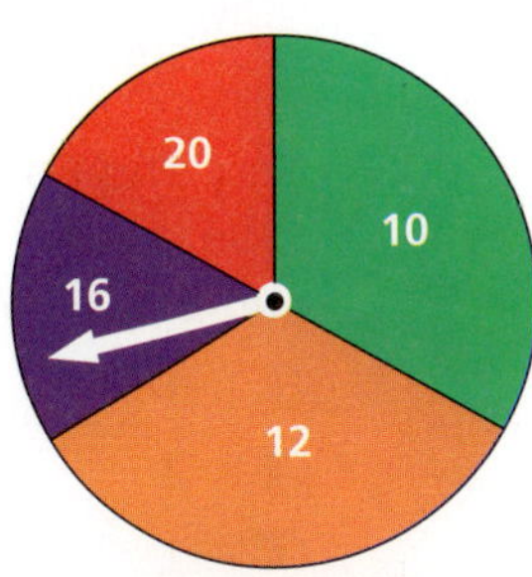

20.

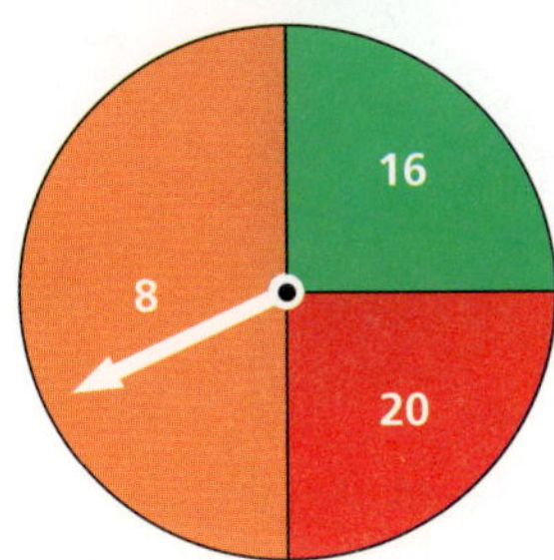

21.

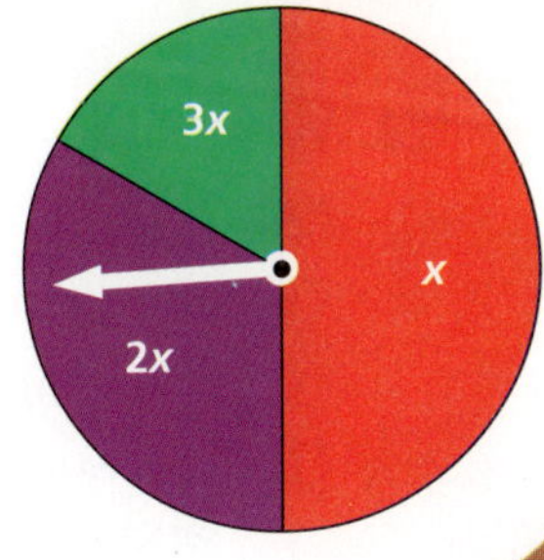

22. **Estimation** Jack has a bag of marbles for a game. There are 30 marbles in the bag, 8 are red, 12 are blue, and 10 are green. Each red marble is worth 5 points, each blue marble is worth 3 points and each green marble is worth 2 points. What is the approximate expected value of picking a marble from the bag?

23. **Write About It** Suppose that an item is insured for \$10,000. The insurance company estimates that there is a 1% chance that they will have to pay out on the policy. If they need to make a profit of 50%, explain what they should charge for the policy.

Photodisc/Getty Images

24. **ERROR ANALYSIS** Camilla estimated the expected value of an 8-sided die with sides labeled 2, 3, 3, 6, 6, 6, 6, and 16 as follows:

$$2\left(\frac{1}{8}\right) + 3\left(\frac{1}{8}\right) + 6\left(\frac{1}{8}\right) + 16\left(\frac{1}{8}\right)$$

$$\frac{2 + 3 + 6 + 16}{8} = \frac{27}{6} \approx 3.4$$

Identify the error in the calculation of the expected value.

25. **Multi-Step** Most of the time, it takes Devon 32 minutes to get from work to his son's school. He has a 40% chance of hitting traffic on his way to pick his son up, which increases his travel time to 58 minutes.

   a. What is Devon's average travel time?

   b. Is the actual travel time for a given trip likely to be close to the average? Explain.

26. Which of the following has the highest expected value?

   Ⓐ number cube with sides 1, 4, 4, 4, 10, 15

   Ⓑ number cube with sides 2, 4, 6, 8, 10, 12

   Ⓒ spinner divided into 5 equal sections labeled 3, 5, 7, 9, 11

   Ⓓ spinner divided in 3 equal sections labeled 10, 10, 30

27. Gary and Ed are playing a game with a six-sided number cube labeled 1-6. If the cube lands on the numbers 1 or 2, they get 1 point. If the cube lands on any other number, they get 4 points. What is the expected value of rolling the number cube?

   Ⓐ 1

   Ⓑ 2

   Ⓒ 3

   Ⓓ 4

28. What is expected value?

   Ⓐ the probability of an event.

   Ⓑ the sum of all possible outcomes.

   Ⓒ the weighted average of outcomes.

   Ⓓ the relationship containing both direct and inverse variation.

CHALLENGE AND EXTEND

29. **Business** A shoe company has sales projections as shown below for three products. What is the expected value of the sales projections, in thousands?

Product	No. of Units Available	Expected Sales (thousands)	Price per Unit
A	450	0.25	$59
B	320	0.60	$79
C	275	0.15	$119

Peter M. Fisher/Corbis

30. **Write About It** Explain a situation in which you can use mathematics to make a decision. What type of mathematics is involved in making the decision?

SPIRAL REVIEW

Solve each system of linear equations. *(Lesson 3-2)*

31. $\begin{cases} 3x + y = -2 \\ -x + 3y = -16 \end{cases}$

32. $\begin{cases} \frac{1}{2}x + 6 = \frac{2}{3}y \\ -y + 4 = -2x \end{cases}$

Classify each system and determine the number of solutions.

33. $\begin{cases} 4y - x = 5 \\ -2x + 3y = 1 \end{cases}$

34. $\begin{cases} -3x - 2y = 4 \\ 8y = -12x + 4 \end{cases}$

Graph each function, and identify its domain and range. *(Lesson 8-7)*

35. $f(x) = \sqrt{x - 3}$

36. $f(x) = 4\sqrt{x^3}$

37. $f(x) = \sqrt{2x + 8}$

38. $f(x) = \sqrt[3]{x^2} - 3$

Find the domain and range of the function shown in each graph.

39.

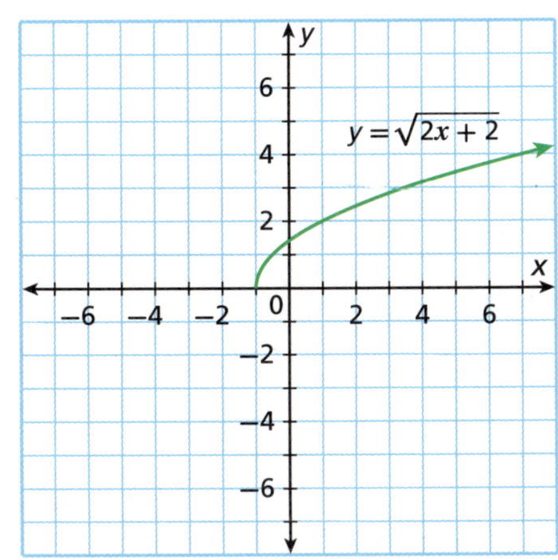

40.

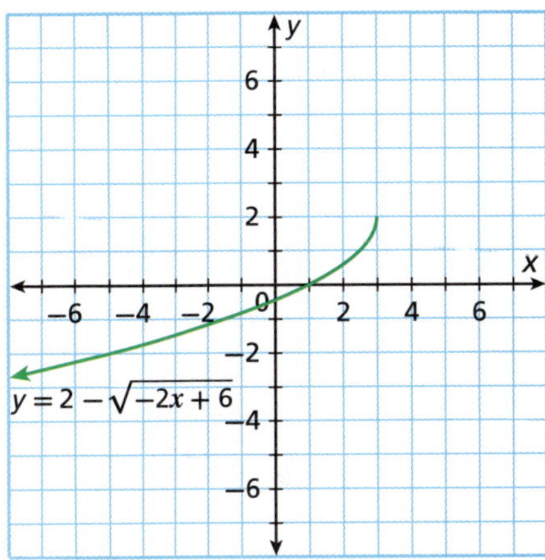

Use constant differences or ratios to determine which parent function would model the data set below. *(Lesson 9-6)*

41.

x	2	3	4	6
f(x)	24	36	48	72

Find the mean, median, and mode of each data set. *(Lesson 11-5)*

42. {3, 8, 10, 18, 10, 5}

43. {11, 13, 23, 22, 14, 11, 29}